DASHIELL HAMMETT

ALSO BY JULIAN SYMONS

FICTION

The Belting Inheritance
The Blackheath Poisonings: A
    Victorian Murder Mystery
Bland Beginning
Bogue's Fortune
The Broken Penny
The Color of Murder
The Delting Secret
The Man Who Killed Himself
The Name of Annabel Lee
The Narrowing Circle
Sweet Adelaide
The Tigers of Subtopia

CRITICISM

Agatha Christie: The Art of Her
    Crimes, the Paintings of Tom
    Adams (with Tom Adams)
Critical Observations
Critical Occasions
The Great Detectives
Mortal Consequences: A History from
    the Detective Story to the Crime
    Novel
The Tell-Tale Heart: The Life and
    Works of Edgar Allan Poe
The Thirties: A Dream Revolved
Thomas Carlyle: The Life and Ideas
    of a Prophet

HBJ ALBUM BIOGRAPHIES
EDITED BY MATTHEW J. BRUCCOLI

ROSS MACDONALD *by Matthew J. Bruccoli*
JACK KEROUAC *by Tom Clark*
JAMES JONES *by George Garrett*
STEPHEN CRANE *by James B. Colvert*
DASHIELL HAMMETT *by Julian Symons*

DASHIELL HAMMETT

by JULIAN SYMONS

HARCOURT BRACE JOVANOVICH, PUBLISHERS

San Diego   New York   London

Requests for permission to make copies of any part
of the work should be mailed to:
Permissions, Harcourt Brace Jovanovich, Publishers,
Orlando, Florida 32887.

Excerpts from The Big Knockover, *edited by Lillian Hellman, are reprinted by permission of Random House, Inc. © Copyright 1962, 1965, 1966 by Lillian Hellman. Copyright 1924, 1925, 1926, 1927, 1929 by Pro-Distributors Company, Inc. © Copyright renewed 1951, 1952, 1953, 1954, 1956 by Popular Publications, Inc.*

Excerpts from The Letters of Nunnally Johnson, *edited by Dorris Johnson and Ellen Leventhal, are reprinted by permission of Alfred A. Knopf, Inc. Copyright © 1981 by Dorris Johnson.*

Illustrations credited to UCLA are from Special Collections, University Research Library, University of California, Los Angeles. Illustrations credited to UCSD are from the Mandeville Department of Special Collections, Ira Wolff Collection, University of California, San Diego. Photographs credited to UTA are reprinted by permission of The New York Journal American Morgue, Harry Ransom Humanities Research Center, University of Texas at Austin. Photographs credited to the San Francisco Public Library are from the San Francisco Archives, San Francisco Public Library. Photographs credited to the New York Public Library are from the Billy Rose Theatre Collection, Performing Arts Research Center, New York Public Library at Lincoln Center, Astor, Lenox and Tilden Foundations.

Library of Congress Cataloging in Publication Data

Symons, Julian, 1912–
Dashiell Hammett.

(HBJ album biographies)
Bibliography: p.
Includes index.
1. Hammett, Dashiell, 1894–1961.
2. Authors, American—20th century—Biography.
3. Detective and mystery stories, American—History and criticism.
I. Title. II. Series.
PS3515.A4347Z87 1985   813'.52[B]   84-12975
ISBN 0-15-123950-9
ISBN 0-15-623956-6 (pbk.)

Designed by Joy Chu
Printed in the United States of America
First edition
A B C D E

CONTENTS

ACKNOWLEDGMENTS

I owe a considerable debt to Mr. Richard Layman, author of *Shadow Man*, who has generously provided me with photocopies of material from his own Hammett collection and has given generous help and information. Martha Ruddy made available to me the script of *The Case of Dashiell Hammett*, the television documentary made for the Public Broadcasting System by KQED-TV, Channel 9, San Francisco. William F. Nolan has been most cooperative in providing some of the illustrations. Matthew J. Bruccoli, editor of this series of critical biographies, has smoothed the way of an Englishman writing about an American novelist. To all of them go my thanks.

CHRONOLOGY

1894   Samuel Dashiell Hammett is born on 27 May in St. Mary's County, Maryland.

1900–01   The Hammett family moves first to Philadelphia, then in 1901 to 212 North Stricker Street, Baltimore. Hammett is enrolled in public school, which he attends until 1908.

1908   In September Hammett attends Baltimore Polytechnic Institute for one semester but is taken away to help his father in business. He has no further formal education.

1909–15   Hammett holds various jobs, none for any length of time. In 1915 he gets a job as an operative with the Pinkerton Detective Agency and holds it until resigning in 1918.

1918   He leaves Pinkerton to enlist in the army on 24 June. He reaches the rank of sergeant.

1919 He is discharged and lives at home until May 1920, when he moves to the Pinkerton branch in Spokane, Washington.

1920–21 In November 1920 he enters the hospital with tuberculosis, is discharged in May 1921, and 7 July marries Josephine Dolan, his hospital nurse. Their daughter Mary is born in October. The Hammetts move to San Francisco.

1922 His first short pieces appear in *The Smart Set*. In December he makes his first contribution to *The Black Mask*.

1923–25 The first Continental Op story appears in *The Black Mask* in 1923. He makes a precarious living by writing for this and other magazines.

1926 His second daughter, Josephine, is born in May. He gives up writing and takes a job with the Samuels Jewelry Company in San Francisco, but gives it up after a few months.

1927 The first installment of *Red Harvest* appears in *Black Mask* in November.

1928 The remainder of *Red Harvest* and *The Dain Curse* appear in *Black Mask*.

1929 Both stories appear in book form and are widely acclaimed. Hammett leaves his family and moves to New York. *The Maltese Falcon* appears in *Black Mask*.

1930 *The Maltese Falcon* is published in book form, and *The Glass Key* appears in *Black Mask*. Hammett goes to work in Hollywood for Paramount and meets Lillian Hellman.

1931 *The Glass Key* is published in book form. Hammett does work for Warner Brothers in Hollywood and then returns to New York. He writes the uncompleted original version of *The Thin Man*.

1932–34 Hammett writes the new version of *The Thin Man*, which is published in book form in January 1934. Film rights are bought by MGM. The film of *The Thin Man* is released with great success. Hammett publishes his last short story.

1935–39 He works as a writer for MGM under a contract which, with some lapses, lasts until July 1939. Films are made from several of his stories, including the first version of *The Glass Key*. In 1937 he becomes involved in left-wing politics. Jose Hammett obtains a Mexican divorce not valid in the United States.

1940–42 Hammett continues to be active in politics. In 1941 the third movie version of *The Maltese Falcon*, with Humphrey Bogart and directed by John Huston, is released and is widely praised. Hammett enlists in the U.S. Army in September 1942.

1943–45 In September 1943, the army assigns Hammett to Alaska, where he edits a daily paper for the troops on the island of Adak. He is discharged in September 1945 with the rank of master sergeant.

1946–51 He teaches mystery writing at the left-wing Jefferson School of Social Science in New York, continues political activities, maintains himself chiefly through radio serials based on his works.

1951 Hammett receives a six-month prison sentence for contempt of court when he refuses to answer questions about a bail fund of which he is chairman. He is released in December. His books go out of print, and his radio shows are taken off the air.

1952–61 Hammett lives primarily in a small gatehouse on a friend's estate in Katonah, New York, sometimes with Hellman on Martha's Vineyard. He writes a small part of a novel called *Tulip*, then gives it up. He is in bad health and extremely poor for almost all this period. On 10 January 1961 he dies in a New York hospital. On 13 January he is buried in Arlington National Cemetery.

1

THE FIRST AMERICAN CRIME WRITER

THE primary achievement of Dashiell Hammett was to create a specifically American brand of crime story and to make it respectable. In the course of doing so he produced at least one novel, perhaps more, that transcends the form and limits of the crime genre and can be compared with the best fiction produced in America between the two world wars.

It is not, of course, literally true that Hammett was the first American crime writer. That was Edgar Allan Poe. But although Poe's five crime short stories show him to be a supreme originator, his interests were so wide that the crime story was to him a comparatively unimportant aspect of his work, interesting chiefly because of the opportunity it gave for his characteristic ingenuity. "People think them more ingenious than they are on account of their method and *air* of method,"[1] he wrote to a friend. Poe's stories in the genre are by intention logical exercises, involving no more emotion than that needed to solve a cryptogram. The American crime writers after Poe followed European models, with one or two exceptions, like Melville Davisson Post (1869–1930), whose Uncle Abner stories are strongly American in their characterizations, scenes, and flavor. Post, like others, however, looked toward Europe as soon as he moved away from Uncle Abner. His further creations, like Sir Henry Marquis, chief of Scotland Yard's Central Investigation Department, and Monsieur Jonquelle, the Paris prefect of police, have a distinctly absurd quality simply because the writer knew little of the background or the people he was describing. Up to the end of World War I, there were almost no truly indigenous American crime or detective novels, although the short stories in O. Henry's *The Gentle Grafter* and George Randolph Chester's *Get-Rich-Quick Wallingford* series are in an American tradition of genial roguery derived from Mark Twain.

The development of pulp magazines after World War I saw the emergence of writers who used the American language rather than the British version of English. They used this language—racy, energetic, powerful, and crude—to create stories about crooks who were ready and eager to use their guns and the equally gun-happy detectives who opposed them. These detectives were rarely policemen, either in or out of uniform, for the pulp writers generally ignored or flouted officialdom and authority. The world they portrayed was much more like that of the real Wild West, where the quickest gun survived.

In most of these stories the writing was as coarse as the characterization. The pulps were regarded by critics as rubbish that nobody interested in literature would read. Yet within a few years of the appearance of his first crime stories in 1923, Hammett was producing work that was obviously beyond the scope of his fellow pulp writers. In part because he had been a Pinkerton detective and so knew the kind of people he was writing about, his work carried a conviction lacking in the stories of those who were merely fantasizing. Many of his crooks were taken from life, and they were not romanticized. Neither was the detective who appears in almost all of these short stories—the fat, extremely tough Continental Op. Raymond Chandler's summary of Hammett's achievement in his essay "The Simple Art of Murder" is witty and accurate:

> Hammett gave murder back to the kind of people that commit it for reasons, not just to provide a corpse; and with the means at hand, not with hand-wrought duelling pistols, curare, and tropical fish. He put

these people down on paper as they are, and he made them talk and think in the language they customarily used for these purposes. He had style, but his audience didn't know it, because it was in a language not supposed to be capable of such refinements. They thought they were getting a good meaty melodrama written in the kind of lingo they imagined they spoke themselves. It was, in a sense, but it was much more.[2]

If Hammett's reputation rested on the Continental Op stories alone, one would say that he was an original writer but not one of the highest talent. He needed the scope and the opportunity of developing character offered by the full-length novel, and it was with the appearance of *Red Harvest* (1929 in book form) that his writing really flowered. The book is as violent as any of the short stories, yet it is far superior to all but the very best of them. It was recognized instantly on its book publication as something new in the crime genre, and also as entirely American. The society, the people, the way they talked and acted, had no relation to Europe.

This separation between the British and the American crime story can hardly be overemphasized. The British story sprang from the genius of Charles Dickens (particularly in the unfinished *Mystery of Edwin Drood* and in *Bleak House,* which introduced the first important professional detective in fiction, Inspector Bucket) and the talent of Wilkie Collins. The British detective was further developed by Sir Arthur Conan Doyle's creation of Sherlock Holmes, and from Holmes came a mass of superman amateur detectives. Hammett was the first writer to break away decisively from this tradition. The figures he created, the Continental Op, Sam Spade, Ned Beaumont, are not amateurs but professionals. They are men of action, not reasoning machines. And they are not superman detectives but men who bleed, suffer, make mistakes—in fact, human beings.

It is on *Red Harvest, The Maltese Falcon* (1930 in book form), and *The Glass Key* (1931 in book form) that Hammett's reputation finally rests. His writing career lasted little more than a decade, effectively ending with the publication of *The Thin Man* (1934). After the first novel Hammett honed his style, so that what had always been spare and hard now also had an edge that allowed sharp comments on the corruption of society, offered a view of the human beings in it that had depth, and was far from idealistic. He perfected an acidity of comment in the use of wisecracks that gave his work a tang absent from that of the two most talented writers who later covered similar ground, Chandler and Ross Macdonald. Hammett worked hard at reducing the violent content in his books, so that even scenes of action tended to be played down rather than up. All this helped him create a new type of hero-villain, a type now common enough in books and films but never rendered with the ambiguity brought to the depiction of Sam Spade and Ned Beaumont.

Further than this, his approach in *The Maltese Falcon* and *The Glass Key* involved an extremely subtle technique of indirection. Intentions are rarely stated; motives are not overt. They have to be inferred, mostly through wonderfully skillful and effective dialogue, occasionally through the interpretation of action. These are novels that ask the constant attention of the reader. They can be taken as straightforward thrillers, but their implications about society and personal relationships, particularly in *The Glass Key*, approach complexities of guilt and innocence quite outside the intent or reach of any ordinary thriller. Other aspects of the three major novels were original in their time, like the treatment of sex, but their lasting quality is that they are not only about violence but make implicit comments on it.

The reasons behind Hammett's silence for more than a quarter-century before his death in 1961 are later discussed in detail. Here it is enough to say that he felt he had come to the end of what he could do with the crime story, and failed in his attempts to write a novel that would throw away what Chandler called the crutch of crime. Hammett created the first truly American crime novels, but he did more than that. *The Glass Key* is a novel that survives comparison with Hemingway and Faulkner. *The Maltese Falcon* contains unforgettable characters. No other book of the period gives violence and corruption the raw reality of *Red Harvest*. The least of his work is interesting; the best has a permanent place in literature.

2

THE EDUCATION OF A WRITER

"I was born in St. Mary's County, Maryland, between the Potomac and Patuxent rivers on May 27, 1894," Hammett wrote. "I was a very fat baby, but grew up tall and thin. The only remarkable thing about my family was that there were, on my mother's side, sixteen army men of France who never saw a battle. That, and the fact that my grandmother went to the movies every afternoon: she loved Wallace Reid."[1]

In later years, as his fame grew, Hammett gave a romantic flavor to much of his youth and early manhood, and there is evidence of it here in his reference to the sixteen army men of France. The assertion came from his mother, Annie, who, although her family name was Bond, had a connection through her own mother with a French family named De Chiell. The middle name of Samuel Dashiell Hammett was a reminder of the aristocratic De Chiells, and she insisted that the emphasis should be on the second syllable—in vain. The boy grew up as Sam; the man was called Dash.

Hammett was "a respected if not entirely respectable name"[2] in southern Maryland in the early and mid-nineteenth century. The Hammetts were traders, sufficiently known and established for the area where they lived to be called Hammettville. Shortly after Dashiell's birth, however, the family fortunes declined. Richard Hammett, his father, was big, handsome, genial, and unsuccessful in almost everything he undertook. He was an aspiring politician who switched parties from Democratic to Republican in a futile attempt to win state office. Then, in the course of moves to Philadelphia and Baltimore, he was manufacturer's agent, streetcar conductor, clerk, and salesman of seafood.[3] Dashiell had just one semester at Baltimore Polytechnic Institute and then left at the age of thirteen to help his father save the business. He failed but he never went back to school. His adult life had begun.

The effect of this erratic upbringing is something about which we can only speculate. He retained throughout his life a sort of disdainful pride that can surely be traced to his mother's influence in those early years. Annie dreamed of the De Chiell grace and courtesy, attributes lacking in the breezy, hard-drinking Hammetts. The strong Catholicism of the Hammetts also played its part—religion was important enough to the family for Richard to have insisted on Annie's converting when they married. And perhaps there should be added to these influences a particular southern feeling for dignity, courage, and style. We know that Dashiell loved his mother and constantly quarreled with his father. In the days of Hammett's fame the two men did not meet, but after World War II Dashiell visited the old man in Virginia and paid for an artificial leg to replace one he had lost from diabetes. Dashiell did not, however, attend his father's funeral, saying that he had paid for it and others could do the crying. It is possible that Richard served as the model for the back-slapping, good-natured, but ultimately corrupt and stupid Paul Madvig in *The Glass Key*.

Yet Dashiell was in many ways his father's son. The fat baby grew up not only tall and thin but also red-haired, reckless, easily angered, fanatically independent. His younger brother, Richard, Jr., had a steady clerking job, but Dashiell moved from one job to another, never staying anywhere long. Richard remembered his brother working as a railroad office boy and for a brokerage house, where he chalked stock market prices on a board from the ticker tape. Although he changed jobs often, he did not leave the family home on Stricker Street in Baltimore. Theirs was a respectable house on a respectable street, even though the street was unpaved and all of the houses had outdoor privies. A woman friend remembered Annie Hammett as the loveliest neighbor she had ever met. But Dashiell, the friend said, didn't inherit his mother's grace and sweetness. He had few companions, and they did not include his brother, who recalled afterward that they did not play together and associated with different sets of people.[4] Walter C. Pohlhaus, who knew him as a boy (Hammett dropped an *h* and used the name for a detective in *The Maltese Falcon*), said that he was quiet and introspective. (He remained so in later years, saying little until his tongue was unlocked by drink.) He used the local library, borrowing mostly mysteries and what his friend Pohlhaus called swashbuckling tales. In his mid-teens he also began to drink and to associate with girls, even though one girl thought he was the ugliest boy she had ever seen. When he was twenty, he got the first of several doses of gonorrhea, the results of which were increasingly damaging to his health. At twenty-one, after answering what he called an enigmatic want ad in a Baltimore paper, he went to work for the Pinkerton Detective Agency. The agency was the biggest of its kind in the country.

There has been more mythmaking about this phase of his career than any other, the myths being encouraged and perhaps in some cases even created by Hammett himself. His service was comparatively brief. He was a Pinkerton man, first as a clerk and then as a field operative, from sometime in 1915 until June 1918, when he enlisted in the army. During this time he was based in the Baltimore office. After his discharge from the army he worked for a few months, probably part-time, in the Spokane branch, and in the following year spent a period that was certainly no more than eight months in the San Francisco office. No doubt he drew on the Baltimore years when he began to write, but San Francisco provided the background for most of his short stories, and the months he spent in the agency office there provide the basis for the picture of Hammett as detective.

Much of what we know about his Pinkerton experience comes from Hammett himself, most memorably in the notes "From the Memoirs of a Private Detective," which he published in 1923. These piquant, epigrammatic notes, none longer than a few lines, tell us that he once had to perjure himself to escape a perjury charge, that he had to give directions to a subject he was shadowing because the man had lost his way, and that house burglary is the worst-paid occupation in the world. He said not only that he had known a man who stole a Ferris wheel but also that he had found it. How? It was simple enough, as he explained later in a newspaper interview. "You don't steal something that big for your back yard. I knew it had to be at another carnival."[5] And sure enough, that was where he found it. The tone of the memoirs is cynical and worldly. Here are some excerpts that suggest the flavor and also demonstrate that Hammett had already developed an individual style:

I know a man who will forge the impressions of any set of fingers in the world for $50.

I have never known a man capable of turning out first-rate work in a trade, a profession or an art, who was a professional criminal.

I know a detective who once attempted to disguise himself thoroughly. The first policeman he met took him into custody.

Pocket-picking is the easiest to master of all the criminal trades. Anyone who is not crippled can become an adept in a day.

The chief of police of a Southern city once gave me a description of a man, complete even to a mole on his neck, but neglected to mention that he had only one arm.

That the law-breaker is invariably soon or late apprehended is probably the least challenged of extant myths. And yet the files of every detective bureau bulge with the records of unsolved mysteries and un-caught criminals.[6]

There seems no doubt that Hammett was a good detective. "He was tall, thin, smart as a steel trap," according to another detective who worked with him in San Francisco.[7] He said himself that he had always found shadowing easy and added that the four rules were to keep behind your suspect, never try to hide from him, act naturally, and never try to meet his eye. He claimed to have followed a suspect for six weeks, riding trains and visiting half a dozen small towns in his company without suspicion. The fellow detective quoted above also said that "Hammett made a good shadow" and that he "rated at the very top" with the San Francisco office. At this time Hammett was probably a free lance. The pay was six dollars a day, a better rate than the twenty-one dollars a week with no overtime pay when he joined in 1915.

It is natural to ask whether Hammett worked on any famous cases, but the answers are doubtful, because they are chiefly based on what he himself said years afterward. The colleague already mentioned confirms that they worked together on the Fatty Arbuckle case. Arbuckle, at the time second only to Charlie Chaplin as a film comedian, was charged in 1921 with killing in the act of rape an actress named Virginia Rappe, and although he was acquitted, the scandal ended his career. Hammett and his colleague worked for Arbuckle's lawyers and shadowed some prosecution witnesses. Hammett claimed as well that he had played a part in the bond theft case involving the gambler Nicky Arnstein, in the arrest of a robber named Gus Schaefer, and in the discovery of more than $100,000 in stolen English sovereigns on board the freighter *Sonoma*. All of the stories are open to question, although one or another may be true. It is significant that when his wife was asked about his detective work at this time, she mentioned none of these assignments, although she remembered that he was a very good shadow man, fell off a taxi on one occasion, and was once hit from behind with a brick so that "there was a dent in the back of his head like the corner of a brick"[8] and he sat still in a chair for two days in the course of recovery. Years later his friend and lover, Lillian Hellman, noticed the dent in his head, and the scars on his legs.

All these tales relate to those months in San Francisco. While working from the Spokane office, he was given an assignment which he talked about less often. The agency was employed by mine owners in Anaconda, Montana, to help in breaking a miners' strike there. When he later told his daughter Mary about having been one of the agents involved, she was incredulous: "You mean you were working for Pinkerton against the I.W.W.?" "That's right," Hammett replied, adding that at that time he was simply out to do his job and "didn't care if his clients were bums."[9]

Of his first and longest period as a Pinkerton man, we know almost nothing. It ended with his enlistment in the army, something he may have done out of patriotism, a desire for adventure, or both. His army service with an ambulance company lasted less than a year, terminated by the onset of the respiratory disease that was to remain with him for the rest of his life. Between bouts in the hospital, he reached the rank of sergeant but eventually was diagnosed as having tuberculosis and given his discharge, with a small pension. He returned to the family home in 1919 as a war veteran who had never seen a battlefront, coughing, hemorrhaging, and so weak that he was barely able to climb a flight of stairs. He recovered, left home again to take the Spokane job, and six months later was admitted to Cushman, the Public Health Service hospital in Tacoma. His weight was down to 132 pounds, and he was now considered totally disabled.

There were two hundred patients in Cushman, suffering from respiratory diseases and shell shock, and the major general in charge ran a permissive regime. There were vocational training classes, but many of the patients were less interested in basket weaving and beadwork than in playing poker and smuggling in liquor. They also flirted with the women vocation instructors and the seven army nurses. Hammett's nurse, who had the rank of second lieutenant, was Josephine (Jose) Dolan. She was three years younger than Hammett, pretty without being beautiful, sensible although not especially intelligent. More than half a century later Jose remembered him standing out from the other patients. She admired the fastidiousness with which he dressed, his neatness, the way he helped other patients. Was he a hellraiser? Certainly not. "He was so quiet you couldn't even know he was there. He was gentle and read and talked to the patients."[10] They visited restaurants, took occasional boat rides. "I thought he was very intelligent and very striking." Then and later, many women found Hammett an extremely handsome, attractive man. He had light reddish hair, soon to go gray, abundant and combed in a pompadour; a good build; and an air of pride and remoteness that distinguished him in any gathering. Hammett was at Cushman for less than four months. After he left, Jose discovered that she was pregnant. They moved to San Francisco and in July 1921 were married. He gave his occupation as "detective." She was a Catholic; he gave no religion. They were married in St. Mary's Cathedral, but in the rectory, not at the altar.

Jose had married a sick man, and a poor one. They had an apartment on Eddy Street, "a plain furnished place," she remembered, with a living room in front, a bedroom, and another small room with a folding bed behind. The place cost forty-five dollars a month furnished, and Hammett's disability pension, which frequently changed and was at that time reduced

Josephine Dolan, Hammett's hospital nurse, became his wife in 1921.

to fifty percent, did not quite pay the rent. It is easy to believe her when she says that they didn't have much money. He did the cooking, she took out the baby, Mary Jane, born that October. He was advised to avoid contact with the baby as much as possible, for fear of infecting her, and he slept in the room with the folding bed, while Jose and Mary shared the bedroom. It was a hard life, practically and emotionally, for all of them. Hammett used the San Francisco library nearby. There he read newspapers and magazines and borrowed books, undertaking a course of reading to supplement his inadequate education. He read omnivorously: scientific and mystery stories, biography and history, the popular fiction of the time, and classic novelists, including Flaubert, Anatole France, and Henry James. He spoke afterward more than once of the debt he owed to James and surprised friends by his detailed knowledge of James's work.[11]

Hammett's health did not improve. His weight went down again, to little more than 130 pounds. At one time, Mary remembered, he had to put chairs across the room so that he could reach the bathroom. In December he was forced to give up the Pinkerton job. A couple of months later he enrolled in a training program provided by the Veterans' Bureau. He learned to type and also to write, in the sense of shaping his sentences coherently and grammatically. He intended somehow to make a living by writing—as a reporter, as an advertising man, as a journalist producing pieces for the magazines, or perhaps as all three.

Hammett was twenty-seven years old. During most of his time as a Pinkerton operative he had retained close links with his family, even living at home for some time. Less than a year after his marriage his mother died, and her death marked an alienation from the rest of the family, particularly from his father. Richard Hammett, Sr., had refused to provide financial support to help Dashiell establish himself as a writer.[12] This was never forgotten, although in the end it was forgiven. Dashiell saw little of his sister, Reba, and nothing of his brother, Richard, Jr. With the death of his beloved mother, he cut himself off from them all.

The prospects of commercial success in any field, or of his living for more than another year or two, looked slim, but there is no indication that either he or Jose ever thought so. In fact, although he did not know it, he had completed his education. In the productive writing life that now began, he used again and again the things that had happened to him and the world he had seen as a Pinkerton agent. He had mixed with crooks of all kinds; he knew the curious interplay, amounting almost to comradeship, that exists between cops and robbers. He had a splendid ear for underworld slang and enjoyed the San Francisco underworld of illicit liquor dealing (the landlady at Eddy Street was a bootlegger) and prostitutes. He was sexually attracted by prostitutes through his life, although at this time he lacked money to pay for them.

If Jose knew or guessed this, she did not admit it. He was always polite, even kind, to her, but however ardent in the first months of their relationship, his feelings cooled rapidly under the stress of living with his new family in something approaching poverty. She was so much his intellectual inferior that they had little in common. Good-natured but commonplace, Jose was not a suitable companion for a man who proposed to make a living by becoming a good, commercially successful writer. They would stay together for another few years, but the marriage was not a happy one.

3

THE SHORT STORIES

W H E N he had become successful, Hammett, in a rare literary pronouncement, made what can be taken as a statement of his creed as a writer:

> The contemporary novelist's job is to take pieces of life and arrange them on paper. And the more direct their passage from street to paper, the more lifelike they should be . . . to make what is set down seem contemporary, to give the impression of things happening here and now, to force upon the reader a feeling of immediacy. . . . He must know how things happen—not how they are remembered in later years— and he must write them down that way.[1]

At first, however, he was far from realizing that these should be his aims or even that the sources of his work must lie in his own experience. He began by trying to write cleverly in the then current sophisticated style that marks the early work of F. Scott Fitzgerald and the novels of Carl Van

Vechten. In a prefatory note to "The Great Lovers," a survey of a dozen historical figures given us in their own egotistical words, he remarked, "I should like to go monthly to some hidden gallery and, behind drawn curtains, burn perfumed candles before [these] images."[2] This worshipful yet iconoclastic aestheticism was distinctly in tune with *The Smart Set*, the magazine founded in 1914 by H. L. Mencken and George Jean Nathan, and it was there that Hammett sold his first short pieces, some of them no longer than five hundred words. "From the Memoirs of a Private Detective," published in *The Smart Set* in 1923, revealed a different, self-assured Hammett, who had outgrown the sense of strain apparent in his apprentice bits and pieces. Perhaps the success of these notes made Hammett aware that his future lay in writing detective fiction. From 1923 onward, detective stories became dominant in his writing, and after a year or two he was producing almost nothing else. At the beginning he made notes and wrote a first draft in his own hand. Later he worked directly on an old Underwood typewriter that belonged to Jose.

The stories were written for the pulps (so called because of the porous gray pulp paper on which they were printed) and most of them for *The Black Mask*, also founded but soon sold by Mencken and Nathan. In the early twenties the detective story was a gentlemanly and ladylike affair, whether the tales were short, like those of Conan Doyle, or full-length, like those of Agatha Christie. The first Christie novel appeared in 1920, and the first by Dorothy L. Sayers in 1923, heralding a legion of genteel women writers. In America the Mary Roberts Rinehart novels, which always at some point found the heroine quivering with fear as she awaited an unknown murderer, were immensely popular. The prevailing short-story mode was still in the pattern set by the Sherlock Holmes tales: an omniscient detective, a puzzle to be solved which had little relation to actual detective work, and a consistent shunning of physical violence.

The pulps were different. They offered what were essentially adventure stories about crime, full of violent action, sometimes but not often including a puzzle to be solved at the end. When *The Black Mask* began publication, it printed detective puzzles side by side with the tougher tales, but these soon faded away. Readers of polite detective stories may have regarded them as existing below the salt, but the pulps were popular. Their heroes bore no resemblance to Hercule Poirot, Lord Peter Wimsey, or even Sherlock Holmes. "Many people have their little peculiarities," said

The Smart Set, *October 1923, contained Hammett's last piece published in the magazine, "The Green Elephant." (UCLA)*

The Smart Set, *October 1922, contained Hammett's first magazine appearance.* (UCLA)

"The Parthian Shot,"
Hammett's first appearance
in print, in The Smart Set,
October 1922 (William F.
Nolan)

The Parthian Shot

By Dashiell Hammett

WHEN the boy was six months old Paulette Key acknowledged that her hopes and efforts had been futile, that the baby was indubitably and irremediably a replica of its father. She could have endured the physical resemblance, but the duplication of Harold Key's stupid obstinacy—unmistakable in the fixity of the child's inarticulate demands for its food, its toys—was too much for Paulette. She knew she could not go on living with *two* such natures! A year and a half of Harold's domination had not subdued her entirely. She took the little boy to church, had him christened Don, sent him home by his nurse, and boarded a train for the West.

Vol. LXIX   OCTOBER, 1922   No. 2

Contents

And Various Burlesques, Epigrams, Poems, Short Satires, Etc.

Manuscripts *must* be addressed, "Editors of THE SMART SET"

No responsibility is assumed for manuscripts that are not accompanied by a fully stamped, self-addressed envelope

The contents of this magazine are protected by copyright and must not be reprinted without permission

YEARLY SUBSCRIPTION $4.00   SINGLE COPIES 35 CENTS

Issued Monthly by the Smart Set Company, Inc., 25 West 45th Street, New York

Entered as second class matter, March 27, 1900, at the Post Office at New York, N. Y., under the act of March 3, 1879

Printed in U. S. A.

Eltinge F. Warner, President and Treasurer   George Jean Nathan, Secretary

Western Advertising Office, Wrigley Building , Chicago, Ill.

The Smart Set is published in England at 265, Strand, London, W. C. 2.

Carroll John Daly's Race Williams, the first of the pulp private eyes. "Mine was holding a loaded gun in my hand while I slept." The pulp writers had some similarities to such British writers as "Sapper," in one of whose books foreign Jewish Communists were "flogged to within an inch of their lives," while in another "there was a sound of a boot being used with skill and strength, and cries of pain," but his Bulldog Drummond was an officer and a gentleman, whereas the pulp private eyes were just doing a job for money.

Pulp writing paid the wretched standard rate of a penny a word, so that making a reasonable living required writing a lot of words. It was hackwork done mostly by hack writers, although in the best pulp stories there was an energy and inventive liveliness lacking in the genteel tales of the period. There was an element in Hammett that did not like what he was doing, so that in letters he referred to himself as producing "the *Black Mask* junk" or "Blackmasking." But another part of him took it seriously and, while acknowledging that the form was trivial, set about trying to use it to say things of interest about American life and society. In some of the early stories written for the pulps, either because he was uncertain about what he was doing, or because he despised it, he used the pseudonym Peter Collinson. A *Peter Collins*, in outdated theater or criminal slang, is somebody nonexistent, a nobody, so that the name means "Nobody's Son." After 1924, however, he worked under his own name.

For these stories he invented a first-person narrator who is known simply as the Continental Op. The Op is short, fat, and expresses few opinions about anything except his job, which he carries out with ruthless efficiency. He works for the Continental Agency and was once said by Hammett to have been based on James Wright, the assistant manager of the Baltimore Pinkerton office.[3] At another time, however, the author claimed that he was more or less a type, and that also may be true. The Old Man, the Op's highly intelligent boss, who has all the sentiment of an adding machine, may have been based in part on Phil Geauque, superintendent of the San Francisco office.

The Op is not married. He is thirty-five and has been at the agency for fifteen years ("The Golden Horseshoe," 1924). We are told in "Dead Yellow Women" (1925) that he lives in an apartment building. And he likes what he does. In "The Gutting of Couffignal" (1925), when refusing a bribe, he says with a rare burst of eloquence: "I pass up about twenty-five or thirty

Arson Plus

By Peter Collinson

(Author of "The Vicious Circle," Etc.)

This is a detective story you'll have a hard time solving before the end. Form your ideas of the outcome as you go along and then see how near you guessed it.

JIM TARR picked up the cigar I rolled across his desk, looked at the band, bit off an end, and reached for a match.

"Fifteen cents straight," he said. "You must want me to break a *couple* of laws for you this time."

I had been doing business with this fat sheriff of Sacramento County for four or five years—ever since I came to the Continental Detective Agency's San Francisco office—and I had never known him to miss an opening for a sour crack; but it didn't mean anything.

"Wrong both times," I told him.

"I get two of them for a quarter; and I'm here to do you a favor instead of asking for one. The company that insured Thornburgh's house thinks somebody touched it off."

"That's right enough, according to the fire department. They tell me the lower part of the house was soaked with gasoline, but God knows how they could tell—there wasn't a stick left standing. I've got Mc-Clump working on it, but he hasn't found anything to get excited about yet."

"What's the layout? All I know is that there was a fire."

25

"Arson Plus," the first Continental Op story, from The Black Mask, *October 1, 1923* (William F. Nolan)

The January 1, 1924, issue of The Black Mask *featured Hammett's "The Tenth Clue." (UCLA)*

WOMEN POLITICS & MURDER

by Dashiell Hammett ~

Mr. Hammett's San Francisco Detective is on the job again, working on a mystery the solution of which is so simple that you'll be ashamed of yourself for not figuring it out. And take our word for it, you won't come within a thousand miles of the explanation—yet this is the most realistic and probable story in the issue.

A PLUMP maid with bold green eyes and a loose, full-lipped mouth led me up two flights of steps and into an elaborately furnished boudoir, where a woman in black sat at a window. She was a thin woman of a little more than thirty, this murdered man's widow, and her face was white and haggard.

"You are from the Continental Detective Agency?" she asked before I was two steps inside the room.

"Yes."

"I want you to find my husband's murderer." Her voice was shrill, and her dark eyes had wild lights in them. "The police have done nothing. Four days, and they have done nothing. They say it was a robber, but they haven't found him. They haven't found anything!"

"But, Mrs. Gilmore," I began, not exactly tickled to death with this explosion, "you must—"

"I know! I know!" she broke in. "But they have done nothing, I tell you—nothing. I don't believe they've made the slightest effort. I don't believe they want to find h-him!"

"Him?" I asked, because she had started to say *her.* "You think it was a man?"

She bit her lip and looked away from me, out of the window to where San Francisco Bay, the distance making toys of its boats, was blue under the early afternoon sun.

"I don't know," she said hesitantly; "it might have—"

Her face spun toward me—a twitching face—and it seemed impossible that anyone could talk so fast, hurl words

67

Continental Op stories from The Black Mask, *September and November 1924* (UCLA)

The GOLDEN HORSESHOE

by DASHIELL HAMMETT

Author of the San Francisco Detective Stories

In our recent voting contest for favorite BLACK MASK *authors, Dashiell Hammett received thousands of votes because of his series of stories of the adventures of his San Francisco detective. He has created one of the most convincing and realistic characters in all detective fiction. The story, herewith, is one of his best to date. We know you'll enjoy it to the last word.*

A Complete Novelette

"I HAVEN'T anything very exciting to offer you this time," Vance Richmond said as we shook hands. "I want you to find a man for me—a man who is not a criminal."

There was an apology in his voice. The last couple of jobs this lean, grey-faced attorney had thrown my way had run to gun-play and other forms of rioting, and I suppose he thought anything less than that would put me to sleep. Was a time when he might have been right—when I was a young sprout of twenty or so, newly attached to the Continental Detective Agency. But the fifteen years that had slid by since then had dulled my appetite for rough stuff. I don't mean that I shuddered whenever I considered the possibility of some bird taking a poke at me; but I didn't call that day a total loss in which nobody tried to puncture my short, fat carcass.

"The man I want found," the lawyer went on, as we sat down, "is an English architect named Norman Ashcraft. He is a man of about thirty-seven, five feet ten inches tall, well built, and fair-skinned, with light hair and blue eyes. Four years ago he was a typical specimen of the clean-cut blond Britisher. He may not be like that now—those four years have been rather hard ones for him, I imagine.

"I want to find him for Mrs. Ashcraft, his wife. I know your Agency's rule against meddling with family af-

37

thousand of honest gain because I like being a detective, like the work. And liking work makes you want to do it as well as you can. Otherwise there'd be no sense to it. That's the fix I am in. I don't know anything else, don't enjoy anything else, don't want to know or enjoy anything else. You can't weigh that against any sum of money."[4] It is likely that Raymond Chandler based Philip Marlowe's sentiments about being a detective in *The Lady in the Lake* on this passage, although Chandler's phrasing is more romantic. A little later in the same story, when a criminal, the Princess, offers to go to bed with him, the Op elaborates his position: "You think I'm a man and you're a woman. That's wrong. I'm a manhunter and you're something that has been running in front of me. There's nothing human about it."[5] And at the end when she walks away, not believing his threat that he will shoot her, he puts a bullet in her leg. "I had never shot a woman before. I felt queer about it."[6]

One of the most interesting things about the stories, which distinguished them from the beginning from the run of pulp fiction, is the way the Op's ethical code is shown to us, shown without being emphasized. The opening sentence of a very early story, "House Dick" (1923), tells us: "The Montgomery Hotel's regular detective had taken his last week's rake-off from the hotel bootlegger in merchandise instead of cash, had drunk it down, had fallen asleep in the lobby, and had been fired."[7] The implications, without a word being positively said to that effect, are that if you are a detective, you should be honest and shouldn't get drunk, and that if you are dishonest and also drunk on the job, it is right that you should be fired. This code of behavior is extended to include all sorts of loyalties connected to the job, as in *The Maltese Falcon*, in which Sam Spade feels the need to be loyal to his partner even though that partner is fairly worthless. Perhaps Hammett learned this ethic from James Wright or Phil Geauque, or perhaps it was simply experience that taught him the need for detectives working together to be loyal to each other, no matter what their fallibility as human beings. The Op's ethic excludes sentiment, and in this, too, he is unusual although not unique among private eyes. In the last line of "The Gutting of Couffignal" he says to the woman he has shot: "You ought to have known I'd do it. Didn't I steal a crutch from a cripple?" And it is true that he has taken a crutch from a one-legged newsboy, although he has left "five bucks for rental."

The creation of the Op, and of a social ethic for him wholly remote from that of other fictional detectives of the period, is the most notable thing about these twenty-odd stories published in 1923 and 1924. They are the work of a writer learning his trade, and the shorter ones, in particular, are no more than efficient hackwork. Hammett needed space in which to develop what became increasingly complex plots. Short stories that depend on an ingenious twist at the end, which he wrote in response to market demand, did not really suit him.

These two years saw Hammett developing the style that by 1927, when he came to write *Red Harvest*, had been perfected. From the first, he used epithets and adjectives sparingly, attempting that direct passage from street to paper. The opening sentence of "House Dick" tells us exactly what we need to know—and no more—about why the Op is doing what he calls hotel-coppering. The style is deliberately without color, taking its tone chiefly from the use of criminal and other slang. Whether or not Hammett intended it at this time, it is a style so bare and dry that it offers the maximum contrast with the violent events in the stories.

The obvious similarity of Hammett's style in these early stories to that of Hemingway's first stories about Nick Adams has prompted arguments about possible influences. Hemingway could not have influenced Hammett, because before 1925 he had published nothing in the United States; and it is not likely that Hammett influenced Hemingway, although there are passages of dialogue in *The Sun Also Rises* (1927) that Hammett might have written. Times of change are often accompanied by shifts in literary style among new writers, and the United States after World War I was a society in turmoil. The new world created by Prohibition, gangsterism, and the loosening of sexual and social codes could not be adequately expressed in the prose of Edith Wharton or Willa Cather. The flat realism of Sinclair Lewis was adequate to the world of Main Street, but neither Hammett nor Hemingway was writing about Main Street or Babbitt. They used a prose which seemed to express naturally the worlds they were depicting: in Hemingway a world sometimes of warfare and often of physical action, in Hammett a violent, brutal, and corrupt sector of society. They eliminated the author's voice as much as possible in an attempt to make the final product genuine and not synthetic—life rather than literature.

One must not claim too much. There is a lot that is conventionally literary in Hammett's early stories, even more that is conventionally violent. At the end of "The Girl with the Silver Eyes" (1924) the girl villain puts her mouth to the Op's ear and whispers "the vilest epithet of which the English language is capable."[8] It is true that we have already been told in "The House in Turk Street" (1924), where she first appears, that "she was as beautiful as the devil, and twice as dangerous."[9] Both of these stories contain some stale literary language. The Op thinks uncharacteristically (and incorrectly) about a couple of elderly homebodies, "These folk weren't made to lie to," and a lawyer tells him about a man who has left his wife, "What was left of his pride would not let him return to her until he looked like his former self." Some British characters are unintentionally caricatured, with drawling voices in which they say things such as "You've the instincts and the intellect of a troglodyte" to fellow crooks.

Yet there are good things, too. The complex plots are finely fitted together to make the characters' actions seem both intelligible and reasonable. This may sound like mild praise, but plotting was of little interest to many of the early hard-boiled writers. The action itself is often described with conviction and with a freshness not easy to achieve. Shooting, stabbing, gouging, and fighting are the conventions of this kind of tale, and it might be thought that one shooting or stabbing is the same as the next. But with Hammett this is not so. He found a marvelous variety of ways in which to say that the Op was near death. "His gunfire cooked my cheek . . . guns blossomed. . . . Rifle bullets sang every which way."[10] Such a skill is, of course, a minor one, a way to make Blackmasking tolerable, Hammett might have said; yet that he took so much trouble to produce these small variations on a constant violent theme shows his difference from the typical magazine contributor. Some of the violent passages are also memorable in their own right, such as the scene in "The Whosis Kid" (1925) in which the Op gets the better of a man who is "big enough and strong enough to play with me"[11] but who makes the mistake of trying to strangle the Op, who then breaks three of his fingers.

The expertise shown in such passages ("You can't choke a man that way—not if his hands are loose and he knows a hand is stronger than a finger") greatly attracted readers of *The Black Mask*, and Hammett was adroit in letting them know that he had personal knowledge of crime, detection, and violence. Most of the details of "The Girl with the Silver

Eyes" he had, he said, either run into personally or learned from other detectives.[12] A particular roadhouse was just as he had set it down; the original of one character had died of tuberculosis in Butte, Montana. When two of his stories were publicly rejected by the editor, his response was also publicized. He said that the rejection had been salutary, that the Op had degenerated into a meal ticket brought out when the landlord, butcher, or grocer was showing signs of nervousness, and he added loftily: "There are men who can write like that, but I am not one of them. If I stick to the stuff that I want to write—the stuff I enjoy writing—I can make a go of it, but when I try to grind out a yarn because I think there is a market for it, then I flop."[13]

Three months later he wrote in the magazine, "For the rest I am long and lean and grey-headed and very lazy." All this impressed readers, but it was far from the reality of Hammett's life. He may have been lazy by nature, but he was industrious by necessity, and far from producing only "the stuff I enjoy writing," he revamped the rejected stories and sold them. He had no choice. He was making no more than $1,000 a year from his stories, and even adding his disability pension and perhaps a couple of hundred dollars made by doing free-lance advertising copy and layout, there was not much money. When he struck lucky with a story, Jose remembered, they had dinner sent in from a restaurant. If money was tight, "I would run a grocery bill for a month or so until a check would come and then I'd take it over and pay."[14] It was not possible to be lazy or to pick and choose.

There are, in all, twenty-six short stories about the Op, plus two linked novellas, "The Big Knockover" and "Blood Money," and two novels, *Red Harvest* and *The Dain Curse*. In the later novels the Op was abandoned. It may be that a figure conceived in short-story terms did not fit happily into longer work, but it is more likely that Hammett felt the need for a character more glamorous than an overweight detective. Yet the Op stories showed a marked increase in skill and sophistication as the author learned his own strengths. None of the stories bears comparison with the best novels, but they have merits of their own.

Hammett's gain in confidence allowed some literary development. His style is noticeably more relaxed from 1925 onward, although in the short stories it is never other than abrasive. Many stories have a dramatic or provocative opening that draws the reader straight into the tale: "It was a wandering daughter job" ("Fly Paper") ; "I was the only one who left the train at Farewell" ("The Farewell Murder") ; "I found Paddy the Mex in Jean Larrouy's dive" ("The Big Knockover") ; "Boiling like a coffeepot before we were five miles out of Filmer, the automobile stage carried me south into the shimmering heat and bitter white dust of the Arizona desert" ("Corkscrew"). These are typical, varied openings. The first two fix the attention irresistibly; the third makes us immediately aware that we are in the heart of gangsterland; the last could hardly be bettered in the brevity with which it conveys place and atmosphere.

The later stories contain the requisite quota of violence and crookedness, but here again Hammett is learning his strengths and weaknesses. Because he never left the United States except for a short visit to Cuba until his service in Alaska during World War II, "This King Business" (1928), about a rich young American who believes he can buy a small Balkan kingdom, is uncertainly handled throughout and ludicrous in some details. As in one or two other inferior tales, Hammett uses the easy technique of setting up the situation through the Op's conversation, so that we are told what we should be shown. Hammett also slowly realized that he was most at home as a writer among professional criminals and that San Francisco, with familiar streets and landmarks identified, provided an excellent backdrop. Readers identified with pleasure the J. M. Wales apartment on Eddy Street in "Fly Paper" and the area through which the Op chased Babe McCloor, and even those who didn't know San Francisco felt the pleasure communicated by an authentic setting skillfully used. In the later stories there are few puzzles to be solved. Generally the Op comes up against crooks prepared to kill for money and plays them off against one another. Some stories end with deadpan abruptness. "Babe McCloor was hanged, for killing Holy Joe Wales, six months later"; "They hanged him"; "If I never have to visit Chinatown again it'll be soon enough." We are introduced with brisk casualness to some of the other Continental operatives: Dick Foley, who talks in telegraphese, wears high heels to increase his height, and uses perfumed handkerchiefs; Mickey Linehan, who "looked like a comedian, and was"; likeable young Jack Counihan, who would "rather catch the wrong man than wear the wrong necktie" and goes down the wrong road in cooperating with the crooks in "Blood Money." Policemen are marginally present but play no important part. The male villains are generally subordinate in cunning and sometimes in viciousness

"Fly Paper" (August 1929) and "The Farewell Murder" (February 1930) were among the last Continental Op stories written for Black Mask. *(UCLA)*

to the women—the Princess in "The Gutting of Couffignal," the girl with the silver eyes in the story of that title, the double-crossing Ines Almad of "The Whosis Kid." Steven Marcus has written about the Op's approach that the reality these women swear to is often fictional: "And the Op's work therefore is to deconstruct, decompose, deplot and defunctionalize that reality and to construct or reconstruct out of it a true fiction, i.e., an account of what really happened."[15] One could put it less portentously by saying that everybody lies to the Op, and to get at the truth he sets one gang against another, plays both ends against the middle.

The stories written in 1925 are longer and better than most of the earlier work. "The Whosis Kid" contains a fine climactic gun battle and the Op's sage reflection when he is in the hands of three villains, all holding guns: "For myself, I counted on coming through all in one piece. Few men *get* killed. Most of those who meet sudden ends *get themselves killed.*"[16] "The Gutting of Couffignal" is a brilliant exercise in deceiving the reader about what exactly happens on the wedge-shaped island that gives the story its title.

"Corkscrew" has a setting unique in the canon, the Arizona desert. The characters are nominally different from the San Francisco thugs the Op most often encounters, although they are no less quick with their guns. Mortality is considerable, and as often in the stories of this period, the main theme has little connection with the battles between Peery and the Circle HAR Ranch that are responsible for most of the deaths. In this story, as in "Dead Yellow Women," written the same year with San Francisco's Chinatown as its setting, the Op plays off rival gangs against each other in a way that anticipates the more complicated deviousness of his activities in *Red Harvest.*

"Corkscrew" has claims to being the best of the stories before the two novellas. Background was important to Hammett, even though he deliberately avoided much descriptive detail, and the atmosphere of almost total lawlessness in which the Op works here has a peculiar veracity. There are well-drawn characters, like the youthful Milk River who first acts as the Op's assistant and then quarrels with him. (The shoot-out between them— "Go for it, fat boy. . . . It's me or you," Milk River cries[17]—is given a characteristic twist by the fact that the Op's gun has a broken firing pin.) There is a girl lunger, or tubercular, again an anticipation of Dan Rolff in *Red Harvest,* who says, "Living out here isn't any different from dying in the big city."[18] And the fight between the Op and an ex-professional gone to seed is among the best things of this kind done by any writer of fiction in the period. It is too long to quote in full, but an extract illustrates its unsentimental and knowledgeable tone:

> I had battled around a little, but there was no doubt that he had me shaded on smartness. To offset that, his hands were lumpy and battered, while mine weren't. And he was—or had been—used to gloves, while bare knuckles were more in my line.
>
> He crouched, waiting for me to come to him. I went, trying to play the boob, faking a right swing for a lead.
>
> Not so good! He stepped outside instead of in. The left I chucked at him went wide. He rapped me on the cheekbone.
>
> I stopped trying to outsmart him, smacked both hands into his body, and felt happy when the flesh folded softly around them. He got away quicker than I could follow, and shook me up with a sock on the jaw.
>
> He left-handed me some more—in the eye, in the nose. His right scraped my forehead, and I was in again.
>
> Left, right, left, I dug into his middle. He slashed me across the face with forearm and fist, and got clear.
>
> He fed me some more lefts, splitting my lip, spreading my nose, stinging my face from forehead to chin. And when I finally got past that left hand I walked into a right uppercut that came up from his ankle to click on my jaw with a shock that threw me back half a dozen steps.
>
> Keeping after me, he swarmed all over me. The evening air was full of fists. I pulled my feet into the ground and stopped the hurricane with a couple of pokes just above where his shirt ran into his pants.
>
> He copped me with his right again—but not so hard. I laughed at him, remembering that something had clicked in his hand when he landed that uppercut, and plowed into him, hammering at him with both hands.

When the fight ends, won by the Op, "His face didn't have a mark on it that I was responsible for. Mine must have looked as if it had been run through a grinder."[19]

Lillian Hellman, introducing a selection of short stories including

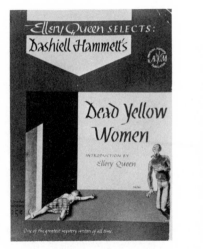

HERE & FOLLOWING PAGE: *Paperback editions of* Black
Mask *stories, published by Spivak, 1943–1951*
(Richard Layman)

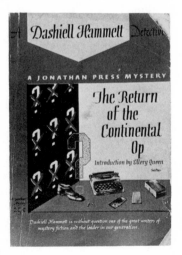
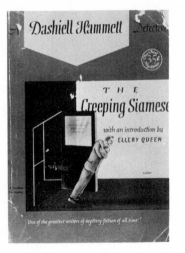

"Corkscrew," said that there had been a time when she thought they were all very good. "But all of them are not good, though most of them, I think, are very good."[20] Hammett sold most of his stories, good or not, but he could not live on the proceeds. Jose was pregnant again, and in May 1926 their second child was born, another daughter, whom they named Josephine. A couple of months earlier Hammett had given up the struggle to make a living by writing stories. He put an advertisement in the *San Francisco Chronicle*, offering to do "any kind of honest work" and adding, "I can write." He was hired by a local jeweler named Albert S. Samuels and was given the grand title of advertising manager.

There is some doubt about the length of time Hammett worked for Samuels, who was, according to his son, "the most wonderful human being on this earth"[21] and was certainly generous to Hammett. Although the best evidence would seem to show that he was with the jeweler for no more than a few months, he left a powerful imprint on the memory of those who met him. Samuels himself recalled that Hammett would write copy all day, go home and drink most of the night, yet report sober the next morning. "He was a man of honor and he always did fine work."[22] The jeweler was particularly pleased by an advertisement showing two young lovers on top of a globe, the girl with a sparkling diamond ring. The copy read: "A Samuels diamond puts you on top of the world."[23] Albert Samuels, Jr., a boy at the time, remembered Hammett's being found by his father and brought to an employees' meeting, after a drinking bout. "He was a salt and pepper gray fellow, thin—almost emaciated looking. He smoked heavy, I'm sure he was a chain smoker. But he seemed to me, looking back, a dynamic and vigorous man."[24] In addition to writing copy and doing layout, Hammett dealt with the mail from customers, which was categorized as either Bouquet or Brickbat. Some letters were used in advertisements, the Bouquets to say thank you, the Brickbats with a promise to do better.

Hammett quickly mastered the technique of advertising and, when Samuels engaged a specialist in the field, took pleasure in arguing with him. "I had a hell of a lot of fun," he wrote Jose. "I hit him with statistics and flourished percentages and the like in his face and quoted all the authorities from Moses to Babson and smothered him with incidents from the experience of the National Biscuit Company and General Motors and sent up assorted facts like fireworks."[25] As this letter shows, he was never on less than friendly terms with Jose, but there is about it a little of the air of an adult writing to enlighten and amuse a child. In fact, their relationship was deteriorating, even though he had a steady job and the family had more money. He drank heavily and began to spend on women. As Jose put it afterward with some delicacy, he drank because people were inviting him out here and there. Samuels, who had strict rules against employees' drinking, was very tolerant, even when Hammett had hemorrhages in the store and was found lying in a pool of blood. Hammett was first given sick leave but was eventually dismissed. The jeweler's good nature, however, prompted one more friendly act. He wrote to the Veterans' Bureau saying that Hammett had resigned his position "because ill health had made it impossible for him to perform his duties."[26] With the return of his tuberculosis, the doctors recommended his absence from the family home for fear of infecting the children. Jose and the girls moved to one apartment, Hammett to another within easy walking distance. Samuels' letter helped to get his disability pension raised again to 100 percent.

It is hard to know what might have happened to Hammett but for the fact that late in 1926 Joseph T. Shaw became editor of *The Black Mask* and made changes in the form of the magazine. Shaw had little knowledge of pulp fiction and did not like much of what he read. He was determined to raise the level of the magazine to make it readily distinguishable from other pulps like *Action Stories* and *Detective Weekly.* Some of his changes were minor, like dropping the definite article in the magazine's title, but one was major. He wanted to encourage his best writers by using them consistently and more often, and to reach this end he was prepared to pay higher rates, something Hammett had been refused early in 1926. Erle Stanley Gardner, another of the chief contributors, had generously offered to accept a cut in his own rate of pay if the money saved went to Hammett, but the idea was rejected by the magazine's owners.[27] Shaw asked Hammett to write for the magazine again and stressed that he did not want puzzle stories of a crossword kind. The reply was enthusiastic: "That is exactly what I've been thinking about and working toward. As I see it, the approach I have in mind has never been attempted. The field is unscratched and wide open."[28]

Shaw gives the impression that he was inaugurating Hammett's career as a hard-boiled writer, but, of course, that was not the case. He was a perceptive editor, however, and it is quite possible that, appreciating the superiority of Hammett's long stories over the shorter ones, he suggested that the writer try his hand at a full-length novel or something near to it, which could be serialized in the magazine. The immediate result, in any case, was the production of two novellas, each nearly twenty thousand words long, "The Big Knockover" and its sequel, "$106,000 Blood Money." They were followed within a few weeks by a novel, *Red Harvest*, which was serialized in four issues. The break with the short story was not complete, but from the time of "The Big Knockover" Hammett evidently considered himself primarily a novelist.

The circumstances of his life changed, including a growing separation from his family. "We moved up to San Anselmo in 1927," his daughter Mary remembered. "Papa stayed in the city writing." He paid them visits twice a week, came at Christmas and spent hours decorating the tree, and, according to Mary, read to her a great deal, all kinds of things, from Edward Lear's "The Owl and the Pussycat" and A. A. Milne's Winnie the Pooh stories to *Crime and Punishment*.[29] Because Mary was only six years old at the time, the accuracy of this recollection is uncertain, but there is no doubt of his love for both girls and his concern for their welfare, a concern that was shown more clearly as they grew up.

Hammett was now alone in San Francisco and enjoying a kind of freedom not possible to him while he lived with Jose. This was roughly the period shown in the film *Hammett* made in 1982 (allowing for a good deal of filmmaker's license), when he had rooms on Post Street and was working, drinking, and becoming involved with people who would be turned into the characters in the books. It is tempting to suppose that this putting aside of marital responsibility was connected with the dramatic improvement in his work, but this is no more than supposition.

The improvement is evident in the novellas. The material they contain is not very different from that of the best among the short stories, although the opening of "The Big Knockover," in which a hundred and fifty crooks are organized to carry out in unison a vast double bank robbery, is elaborated with brilliant skill. What makes the tale memorable, however, is the rich detail provided about the crooks, the use of gangland idioms and phrases which have a wonderful air of reality even though some may have been invented, and the slang that gives a powerful spice to the whole. Hammett's enjoyment of what he was doing is apparent in the Op's listing of what he calls a Who's Who in Crookdom, all of them slaughtered on the

Dashiell Hammett, ca. 1927 (Richard Layman)

instruction of a mysterious Mr. Big after they have carried out the robbery:

> There was the Dis-and-Dat Kid, who had crashed out of Leavenworth only two months before; Sheeny Holmes; Snohomish Shitey, supposed to have died a hero in France in 1919; L. A. Slim, from Denver, sockless and underwearless as usual, with a thousand-dollar bill sewed in each shoulder of his coat; Spider Girrucci wearing a steel-mesh vest under his shirt and a scar from crown to chin where his brother had carved him years ago; Old Pete Best, once a congressman; Nigger Vojan, who once won $175,000 in a Chicago crap-game—*Abacadabra* tattooed on him in three places; Alphabet Shorty McCoy; Tom Brooks, Alphabet Shorty's brother-in-law, who invented the Richmond razzle-dazzle and bought three hotels with the profits; Red Cudahy, who stuck up a Union Pacific train in 1924; Denny Burke; Bull McGonickle, still pale from fifteen years in Joliet; Toby the Lugs, Bull's running-mate, who used to brag about picking President Wilson's pocket in a Washington vaudeville theatre; and Paddy the Mex.[30]

For almost the first time one feels that the author is truly enjoying his creations, alive and dead, and the way they behave. The dialogue, sharp and quick as usual, assumes considerable knowledge among the readers. Familiarity with slang—"nose-candy" for cocaine, "goose" for homosexual, "arch-gonnif" for mastermind—is taken for granted. The very names of the villains, Bluepoint Vance, Happy Jim Hacker, Fat Boy Clarke, Tom-Tom Carey, reek of actuality, as, of course, does that list of corpses, and even Papadopoulos, the mastermind, is a fine creation. The wisecracks remind us that Hammett was Chandler's equal in this American way of turning a phrase. A room is "black as an honest politician's prospects" (Chandler called another room "black as Carrie Nation's bonnet"); Dick Foley talks "like a Scotchman's telegram"; a fight is "a swell bag of nails"; the Old Man has "as much warmth in him as a hangman's rope." The jokes have an acidity peculiar to Hammett, as when Tom-Tom Carey tells the Op that his con-man brother, Paddy the Mex, when "dirty with fifteen thousand or so he'd just nicked somebody for," was foolish enough to give Tom-Tom the money to hold: "That's the kind of hombre he was. . . . He'd trust even his own brother."[31] The acidity fits the characters, for this world is one in which they make no distinction between truth and lies. As Steven Marcus says, we should not trust anything they say more than the Op does, for they tell him whatever seems most advantageous to them at any particular moment.

The Op's behavior becomes steadily more vicious, callous—or realistic. (The terms are optional.) In "The Big Knockover," we are shocked when he shoots a crook named Red O'Leary in the back, because O'Leary has been shown as a comparatively sympathetic character. Red does not know who shot him, and the Op's object is to make contact with the crook's companions. The Op reflects: "Bulldozing a man who might after all be dying wasn't gentlemanly, but I had invested a lot of trouble in this egg, trying to get him to lead me to his friends, and I wasn't going to quit in the stretch."[32] It is not only the Old Man who, in the Op's phrase, can spit icicles in July.

A minor but amusing example of the assurance with which Hammett was now handling dialogue comes when the Op tells Tom-Tom Carey that he is being tailed by a barber named Arlie, and then awaits results. They come in the form of a call at 3:00 A.M. from Dick Foley.

> My bedside phone took my ear out of the pillows. The voice that came over the wire was the Canadian op's.
> "Exit Arlie," he said.
> "R.I.P.?"
> "Yep."
> "How?"
> "Lead."
> "Our lad's?"
> "Yep."
> "Keep till morning?"
> "Yep."
> "See you at the office," and I went back to sleep.[33]

These two stories are the work of a writer who has perfectly mastered the form he is using. Their limitation is that they permit, or the author permits himself, so little in the way of characterization and comment. At Shaw's insistence, Hammett increased the violent action and the number of deaths in the stories, but there is something lacking in stories which say no more than this is the way such people behave, take it or leave it. They have something of the empty brutality of the world they describe. Whether or not Hammett felt this, he now moved to work that offered social criticism of the world he was depicting, the more devastating because it was mostly implicit. He was writing at a time when the gangs were in their heyday, when Capone and his rivals in large measure controlled Chicago. He was ready to write about a town, not Chicago but a town of fair size, that was run by and for the benefit of crooks.

4

RED HARVEST

THE setting of *Red Harvest* is Personville, a town in the Northwest based on Anaconda, Montana, Jose's hometown. Hammett knew Anaconda from his work as a Pinkerton detective and was probably there when open war broke out between the mining corporations and the unions. He told his daughter he was there as a "union-buster," a role for which Pinkerton operatives were often used. Hammett said later that he had turned down an offer of $5,000 by an official of the Anaconda Copper Mining Company to murder a union organizer named Frank Little. Later, Little was lynched, apparently by vigilantes. The struggle between company and unions continued for years. In 1920 fifteen pickets were shot by thugs (not Pinkerton men) brought in by the corporation; the miners on strike were forced back to work, and the imported thugs themselves began to pose a problem for the corporations.[1]

It is significant that Hammett begins his novel with the thugs in control of Personville and does not concern himself with the industrial struggle. Although Bill Quint, the organizer for the International Workers of the World (IWW), who appears early on in the book, says, "I run 'em here," he has no real power in the town, where competing mobs are struggling for supremacy. Quint plays only a tiny part in the story, because the book is not a novel about the battle between management and labor but a thriller.

Yet as we are aware from the beginning, *Red Harvest* is emphatically a story of power and corruption. We learn on the first page that Personville is known as Poisonville and that the police are unshaven, lack buttons on their uniforms, and direct traffic while smoking cigars. In the opening chapter, Quint gives a rundown of the defeat of the striking miners by Elihu Willsson, kingpin of the town, with the aid of hired gunmen. "When the fight was over he couldn't get rid of them. . . . They had won his strike for him and they took the city for their spoils."[2] Quint describes the leading gangsters: Pete the Finn, who handles bootleg liquor; Lew Yard, who has a loan shop and is thick with Chief of Police Noonan; and a gambler named Max Thaler, known as Whisper. The gangsters run the town, nominally for Willsson but really for themselves, with or without his consent. On the day of the Op's arrival, Willsson's son Donald, a civic reformer who is the Op's client, is shot to death.

The form of the story is one Hammett often used. The Op foments trouble between the gangsters, discovers a few dirty secrets, uses them adroitly, and plays every situation to create the maximum violence. In the end all three gangsters are dead, and so is Noonan. *Black Mask*'s final installment of the book is called "The 19th Murder," and a total of two dozen murders take place. Except for the increased violence, which can in part be attributed to Shaw's insistence on action, the book's outline resembles that of some earlier stories, particularly that of "Nightmare Town" (1924). The plot, which appears more intricate than it is because we can never take any statement at face value, is efficient but nothing more. Yet the novel represents an extraordinary advance in its characterization, its perceptions, and, to a lesser degree, its language.

In characterization Hammett gives full play for the first time to his strong visual sense. Here is old Willsson, "the czar of Poisonville":

The old man's head was small and almost perfectly round under its close-cut crop of white hair. His ears were too small and plastered too

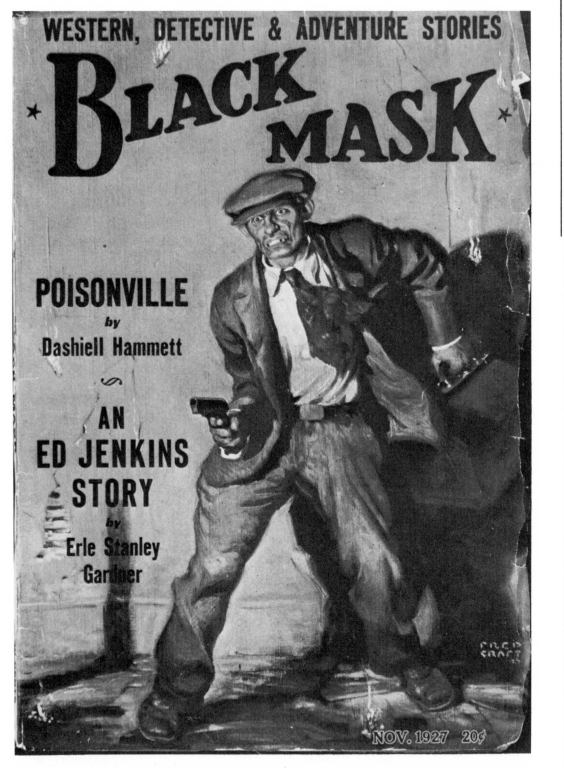

Part I, "The Cleansing of Poisonville," of Red Harvest, *featured in* Black Mask, *November 1927 (UCLA)*

BLACK MASK

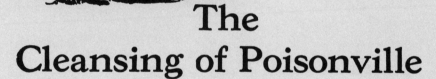

The
Cleansing of Poisonville

By DASHIELL HAMMETT

In recent years there have been too many examples where civic
politics has degenerated into a business for profit. This story is
the first, complete, episode in a series dealing with a city whose
administrators have gone mad with power and lust of wealth.
It is, also, to our minds, the ideal detective story—the new type
of detective fiction which Black Mask is seeking to develop.
You go along with the detective, meeting action with him,
watching the development as the plot is unfolded, finding the
clues as he finds them; and you have the feeling that you are
living through the tense, exciting scenes rather than just reading
a story. Poisonville is written by a master of his craft.

I FIRST heard Personville called Poisonville in 1920, in the Big Ship in Butte, by a red-haired mucker named Hickey Dewey. But he also called his shirt a shoit, so I didn't think anything of what he had done to the city's name. Later, when I heard men who could manage their r's give it the same twist, I still didn't see anything in it but the meaningless sort of humor that used to make richardsnary the thieves' word for dictionary. In 1927 I

Part I of Red Harvest, Black Mask, *November 1927* (William F. Nolan)

flat to the sides of his head to spoil the spherical effect. His nose also was small, carrying down the curve of his bony forehead. Mouth and chin were straight lines chopping the sphere off. Below them a short thick neck ran down into white pajamas between square meaty shoulders. One of his arms was outside the covers, a short compact arm that ended in a thick-fingered blunt hand. His eyes were round, blue, small and watery. They looked as if they were hiding behind the watery film and under the bushy white brows only until the time came to jump out and grab something. He wasn't the sort of man whose pocket you'd try to pick unless you had a lot of confidence in your fingers.[3]

Everything is clearly seen and exactly noted, as though the subject were sitting for his portrait. Hammett pays particular attention to physical detail and clothing, but much less to furnishings, which tend to be ignored or dismissed with a stylish phrase, or to natural surroundings. The gangsters themselves are dealt with briskly, although Whisper's appearance, "young, dark and small, with pretty features as regular as if they had been cut by a die,"[4] hints at the homosexuality that was to be made explicit in Joel Cairo and the young gunman Wilmer of *The Maltese Falcon*. Homosexuality was a subject little dealt with in novels of the period and almost unknown to hard-boiled fiction. As far as we know, Hammett had no special feelings against homosexuals, although Cairo and Wilmer are treated with amused contempt.

Red Harvest contains Hammett's first convincing treatment of a female character. In the early stories the women in central roles are conventionally attractive, conventionally wicked. Their strong, slender bodies become those of lean, crouching animals. They are round-eyed and innocent-looking, but quick with a knife, or red-haired she-devils with little sharp teeth, who may offer the Op a share in the loot or the use of their body. Dinah Brand is altogether different, a figure deliberately created against type. The Op is told that she is a deluxe hustler, a soiled dove, a woman greedy for money but fatally attractive to men. When he meets Dinah, he finds that she has "the face of a girl of twenty-five already showing signs of wear,"[5] with little lines crossing the corners of her big, ripe mouth and around her thick-lashed, slightly bloodshot eyes. Her coarse brown hair needs trimming, her mouth is rouged unevenly, her dress gapes where fasteners have popped open (later she wears a dress with a two-inch rip in one shoulder seam), and there is a run down the front of one stocking. Because, rather than in spite, of these things, her sexual attraction is wholly credible.

Dinah is a tremendous drinker who will do almost anything for money. She sells the Op secrets which he uses to destroy Noonan. To talk of her being in love with anybody would be a bad joke, but she finds the Op a good drinking companion and is fascinated by a mind more devious than her own. In one of the book's most famous scenes, the two drink themselves unconscious with gin and laudanum, and he wakes to find her dead, with her own ice pick buried in her. During the drinking session the Op admits that he is becoming "blood-simple like the natives. . . . 'I looked at Noonan and knew he hadn't a chance in a thousand of living another day because of what I had done to him, and I laughed, and felt warm and happy inside. That's not me. I've got hard skin over what's left of my soul, and after twenty years of messing around with crime I can look at any sort of a murder without seeing anything in it but my bread and butter, the day's work. But this getting a rear out of planning deaths is not natural to me.' "[6]

"Getting a rear" is a slang term meaning in general terms obtaining excitement, so that Dinah offers "an honest to God rear" from gin spiked with laudanum, but it also refers to sexual excitement, something that eluded the strict censorship of the period. The Op does not go to bed with Dinah, but when he wakes, holding the handle of the ice pick that is in her breast, he does not know—and neither do we—whether he has killed her in laudanum-ridden despair. Dick Foley is so horrified by the Op's behavior that, when asked by the Op if he thinks his colleague is a murderer, he can only reply that if he isn't, this would be a good time to say so. And indeed, by any ordinary ethical standard there is little to choose between the Op and the gangsters he destroys. His treatment of an ex-policeman named MacSwain is particularly callous in its cold-bloodedness.

The Op's development was foreshadowed in some of the short stories, particularly "The Gutting of Couffignal," but is still not fully understood. Leslie Fiedler's observation, typical of other critical reactions, that in Hammett's work "the blameless shamus is also the honest proletarian, illuminating the decadent society of the rich,"[7] makes assumptions about the Op and his detective successors that are not justified. The Op is not in any meaningful sense proletarian, and none of the novels touches on "the decadent society of the rich." In regard to Personville, the point is that everything and everybody are corrupt: the police, the gangsters, Dinah Brand, old Elihu Willsson. The only possible exceptions are Donald Willsson, who is killed before the story begins, and the union organizer Quint, who is powerless. And the Op's promise, or threat, to Elihu that he will carry out "a good job of city-cleaning"[8] is not fulfilled. At the end he has cleared out the gangsters, but what will follow? The city is "all nice and clean and ready to go to the dogs again," and Elihu will simply be "pushed around by somebody else."[9] The Op has provided a temporary remedy, not effected a cure, and the means he has used are as vicious as those of his opponents.

The language of *Red Harvest* is rich and colorful. Chandler added to the tribute quoted in Chapter One that Hammett's style was one "which does not belong to Hammett or to anybody, but is the American language," although he remarked also that the language "can say things he did not know how to say or feel the need of saying. In his hands it had no overtones, left no echo."[10] It is surprising that many later critics have accepted this as fair comment. Chandler may have been thinking in part about the fact that Hammett did not create (and would not have wished to create) an idealized figure like Philip Marlowe but would have thought that, in Ross Macdonald's phrase, "down these streets a mean man must go." That the detective is a flawed human being and that it would be absurd to show him as a knight in shining armor was an idea from which Hammett never swerved. He emphasized this a few years later in an introduction to the Modern Library edition of *The Maltese Falcon*, saying that Sam Spade was the kind of figure private detectives liked to think they were.

With regard to *Red Harvest* and the work that succeeded it, the notion that the language has no overtones and leaves no echo is very much astray. Chandler's language, in particular his dialogue, is always good, but it is sometimes too literary, while Hammett's is as raw as his characters' lives. This is particularly evident in the use of slang and colloquial phrases. A glance through half a dozen pages yields *slated for the chutes, he made the sneak, a pork-and-beaner, a ducat back to Philly,* and *it's a gut,*[11] and samplings elsewhere show phrases similarly rich in their allusiveness. This language of the street, racetracks, and poolroom is perfectly fitted to a story whose savagery reflects something in the author's character. There are a lot of jokes in the book, but they are all bitter. Dinah remarks that all of Polly de Voto's bootleg liquor is good except perhaps the bourbon, which "always tastes a little bit like it had been drained off a corpse." While holding a gun to a man's eye the Op threatens to "make an opening in your head for brains to leak in," and he answers a question about the whereabouts of the members of a reception committee by saying that they "probably stopped to get a rope." When Dinah suggests that they should go away for a couple of days together, he replies: "Can't, sister. Somebody's got to stay here to count the dead." The book's ironies are the more effective because of their understatement. When Whisper and the Op are holed up in Whisper's joint, surrounded by police, the gangster simply gives one of his men money to buy their way out. A cop holds the back gate open, and they speed away in a black car, which drops off the Op at his hotel. "The last I saw of it was its police department plate vanishing around a corner."[12] *Red Harvest* is a strongly moral book in its exposure of civic corruption, but the view of humanity behind it is not an elevated one.

The story delighted Shaw and *Black Mask* readers, and perhaps it was this approval that prompted Hammett to send the manuscript to a publisher. It went to the house of Alfred A. Knopf, with an accompanying letter which began: "Gentlemen. Herewith an action-detective novel for your consideration. If you don't care to publish it, will you kindly return it by express, collect."[13] He mentioned that he had been a Pinkerton man "for a number of years," and he listed the places in which his work had appeared.

The "action-detective" novel was not at that time highly regarded by book publishers. W. R. Burnett's *Little Caesar* was still in the offing; James M. Cain's *The Postman Always Rings Twice* lay five years ahead; and both Burnett and Cain regarded themselves as novelists, not writers of mere "action-detective" fiction. But Hammett had been lucky in his choice. Both Alfred Knopf and his wife, Blanche, had keen noses for what was new, and they smelled not only an interesting novel but a kind of work that might become popular. Blanche Knopf asked for revisions, in particular less violence, and called *Poisonville* a hopeless title. But her letter was enthusiastic, and she asked: "Won't you tell me something about your ideas for detective stories, and whether you have any more under way?"[14]

Hammett cut out a couple of murders and suggested several new titles, from which *Red Harvest* was chosen.

Hammett seems also to have been fired into positive enthusiasm for what he was doing by Blanche Knopf's encouragement. There was always part of him that despised what he called the *"Black Mask* junk." He sometimes adopted, as did Chandler a few years later, the attitude of a literary man stooping to work in a low-grade medium. The reviews of crime stories that he wrote from 1927 to 1929 for the *Saturday Review of Literature* are often scathing in their condemnation of highly esteemed works in the genre. He was particularly hard on S. S. Van Dine, whose books about the superlatively gentlemanly and snobbish Philo Vance were the best-selling detective stories of the decade: "His conversational manner is that of a high-school girl who has been studying the foreign words and phrases in the back of her dictionary."[15] He also published some bad poems and a review of a short tale by the now almost forgotten but then famous James Branch Cabell, which in its uncharacteristically worshipful tone suggests his own yearning to be regarded as a real writer.[16] Perhaps, after all, this might be done through the action-detective story. He wrote to Blanche Knopf: "I'm one of the few . . . people moderately literate who take the detective story seriously. I don't mean that I necessarily take my own or anybody else's seriously—but the detective story as a form. Some day somebody's going to make 'literature' of it (Ford's *Good Soldier* wouldn't have needed much altering to have been a detective story), and I'm selfish enough to have my hopes."[17] He also wrote of "adapting the stream-of-consciousness method, conveniently modified, to a detective story," although he never attempted this.

The book, dedicated to Shaw, was published early in 1929, and although it was not a best-seller, the reviews were extremely friendly. There was general recognition that the world it depicted provided an extraordinary contrast to that of Van Dine's aristocratic amateur or that of the equally learned and languid Ellery Queen, who also made his first appearance in 1929. Van Dine, Queen, and the gentlemanly British detective story retained their popularity, but there was an understanding that Hammett offered something new. One reviewer said that the book was "the liveliest detective story that has been published in a decade"; another marked it A plus before finishing the first chapter; most praised its authen-

Part III, "Dynamite," of Red Harvest, Black Mask, *January 1928* (UCLA)

Red Harvest *published by Knopf, February 1929* (Richard Layman)

ticity. More than one reviewer made comparisons with Hemingway. There was occasional deprecation of the author's determination "to make his readers wade in gore and in the slime of the worst criminal life,"[18] but such voices were in a small minority. The first edition sold out during the year, and Knopf must have been well pleased.

Over the years a rising chorus of admiration, much of it outside the United States, has acclaimed the book's subtlety as well as its extraordinary vigor. In England Cyril Connolly listed it as one of the indispensable books of the period and referred to "the American novelists, Hemingway, Hammett, Faulkner, Fitzgerald, O'Hara" as representatives of their time.[19] André Gide read it with astonished pleasure in 1942, admitting: "In English, or at least in American, many subtleties of the dialogue escape me; but in *Red Harvest* those dialogues, written in a masterful way, are such as to give pointers to Hemingway or even to Faulkner. . . . In that very special type of thing it is, I really believe, the most remarkable I have read."[20] In the United States similar recognition has been much tardier or has not been given at all. Edmund Wilson considered James M. Cain much the best of what he called "the boys in the back room." Hammett, he said, was "as far below the rank of Rex Stout as Rex Stout is below that of James Cain," and *The Maltese Falcon*, which he had just read for the first time in 1944, "seems not much above those newspaper picture-strips in which you follow from day to day the ups and downs of a strong-jawed hero and a hardboiled but beautiful adventuress."[21]

Wilson was rarely so imperceptive. It would seem that he was repelled by the very qualities in Hammett's work that attracted not only a mass of readers but other highbrow critics: the acceptance and deliberate use of violence and the rejection of all content that would get in the way of the direct passage of pieces of life from street to paper. The English critic A. Alvarez characterizes the approach precisely in a passage that applies to all Hammett's work, but particularly to the Op stories and *Red Harvest*: "It is his steady refusal to expect anything beyond the immediate, and usually rather nasty, situation, or to presume on any values anywhere, that makes for the curious distinction of his style: the wit, the flair for essential details, the suppressed, pared-down, indifferent clarity. His achievement is to have evolved a prose in which the most grotesque or shocking details are handled as though they were matters of routine, part of the job."[22]

The time following Knopf's acceptance of *Red Harvest* was one of

WESTERN, DETECTIVE & ADVENTURE STORIES

BLACK MASK

Black Lives
By DASHIELL HAMMETT

The Sky Trap
By RAOUL F. WHITFIELD

NOV. 1928-20

Part I, "Black Lives," and Part III, "Black Honeymoon," of
The Dain Curse *in* Black Mask, *November 1928 and*
January 1929 (UCLA)

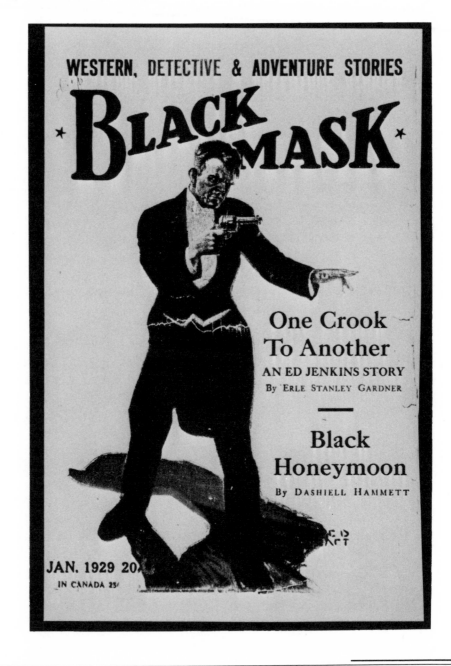

intense industry for Hammett. During 1928 he wrote his second novel, *The Dain Curse*, which was also the last Op novel. Again this was the lead story in four issues of *Black Mask*, and although the editor at Knopf felt less enthusiasm than he had for the first novel, the firm agreed to publish the book. It appeared in July, five months after *Red Harvest*, and the sales were better, two new printings being called for in August. It is likely that the excitement caused by the first book had its effect on the sales of the second.

The Dain Curse is much the weakest of the five novels. Hammett later called it a silly story, and it is easy to agree with him. The central figure is a woman named Gabrielle Leggett, who believes she has inherited a family curse which makes her a corrupting influence, particularly in relation to sex. The character who turns out to be the villain, a novelist named Owen Fitzstephan, is "a long, lean, sorrel-haired man of thirty-two, with sleepy gray eyes, a wide, humorous mouth, and carelessly-worn clothes; a man who pretended to be lazier than he was."[23] Physically, he was a deliberate self-portrait. Fitzstephan's object, so far as it can be discerned in the labyrinth of the plot, is complete domination of Gabrielle. It is a nice, typical Hammett touch that Fitzstephan is an old acquaintance of the Op, so that we are inclined to accept him at face value as a man with "a lot of what seemed to be accurate information and original ideas on any subject that happened to come up,"[24] and as a generally agreeable fellow. Yet much of the action can only be called ludicrous, in particular the scenes relating to the drugged Op's battles in the Temple of the Holy Grail against what he believes to be a ghost immune to revolver bullets. The critic John Bartlow Martin wrote that in the course of the action the Op "shot and stabbed one man to death, helped shoot another dead, was himself attacked with dagger, gun, chloroform, and bomb, fought off a ghostly manifestation barehanded, wrestled with five women, cured a girl of narcotic addiction, and in addition was obliged to deal with one seduction, eight murders, a jewel burglary, and a family curse."[25]

Yet *The Dain Curse* is a less violent book than *Red Harvest*. Why is it also less convincing? In part because, at Shaw's insistence, Hammett made each of the four installments more or less self-contained. At the end of the first installment (the end of Chapter Seven of the book) the magazine announced the second as "a further incident in the 'black life' of Gabrielle Leggett,"[26] and although linking passages were provided, the shift from one theme to another was awkward. Another reason for the book's failure is the

The Dain Curse, *published by Knopf, July 1929*
(Richard Layman)

absence of professional criminals and of any political theme. Hammett was at home writing about gunmen, swindlers, crooks of all kinds, and always dealt knowledgeably with local politics. His touch was much less sure with family curses and erotic religious cults.

There is also a softening, almost a sentimentalizing, of the Op's character, which may have been deliberate but which weakens the story. His rejection of the Princess in "The Gutting of Couffignal" is brusque, but his refusal of Gabrielle is far from that. After he has cured her of drug addiction, reassuring her more than once that she is perfectly normal and that her lack of interest in sex is a not uncommon result of drug taking, she asks: "Why did you go through all this with—for me?" His answer has a sort of avuncular amorousness: "I'm twice your age, sister; an old man. I'm damned if I'll make a chump of myself by telling you why I did it, why it was neither revolting nor disgusting, why I'd do it again and be glad of the chance."[27] A similar scene was to be written much more successfully and credibly in *The Maltese Falcon*.

Although the book is a failure, it is not without interest or merit. It was dedicated to Samuels, the friendly jeweler, and contains a number of in-jokes that must have amused him, including naming characters after company employees. It also incorporates some of the knowledge of diamonds that Hammett had picked up in his advertising job. There are several characteristic bits of repartee, such as the Op's response to Fitzstephan after being reproached for not accepting a set of the novelist's books as a gift: "I was afraid I'd read them and understand them, and then you'd have felt insulted."[28] It is appropriate that this story of middle-class characters includes less slang than the earlier novel dealing with professional crooks, but *The Dain Curse* still contains many of those phrases that seem almost Hammett property, like Mickey Linehan's question to the Op about Gabrielle: "How do you figure her—only fifty cards to her deck?"[29] And comparison between the magazine text and the book version shows that the changes Hammett made, like Chandler's in his later cannibalizing of early stories, were almost invariably improvements. Some are very minor, yet not trivial. In the first paragraph the "shining" diamond was originally "sparkling," and the phrase "searching the lawn as closely as I could without going at it on all fours" was "examining the lawn as thoroughly as I could without going at it on hands and knees." There are eight other corrections on this opening page, none of great importance in itself, that add speed and naturalness to the narrative. "Literary" words and phrases are replaced, particularly in dialogue, by those comparatively colloquial or more easily said. "Mrs. Leggett's dead, I think, but you'd better see if there's any chance. She's on the stairs" becomes "Better take a look at Mrs. Leggett. She's on the stairs. Dead, I think, but you'd better take a look." On the same page the Op's brisk exchange with Collinson—" 'I hope you're satisfied with the way your work got done.' 'It got done,' I said"— originally included the needless adverb "stubbornly" and twenty additional lines that weakened its effectiveness.[30] Although he cut some violence and one killing, Hammett could do little to revise the book's melodramatic structure, but the textual changes sharpen effects and make some individual scenes more plausible.

The novel also gives us for the first time a sexually attractive young woman as a victim. The suggestion has been made by Richard Layman that in Hammett "aberrant sexual behavior, whether homosexuality, a woman's use of sex to control and destroy men, or a man's attempt to stifle the sexuality of a beautiful young woman, was synonymous with criminality," and that sexuality in his work is most often a mark of corruption and "represents the extent to which a character has departed from a romantic ideal of man's capacity for uncorrupted love."[31]

This seems wide of the mark. Hammett's treatment of sex in fiction was consistently outspoken for the period and was soon to become outstandingly so. It is true that the Op does not bed any of the women who tempt him, but this is because of adherence to a professional ethic and no other reason. He does not regard "a woman's use of sex" as something evil but simply feels that emotional complications might stop him from doing his job as well as it should be done. This was probably something like Hammett's own attitude. Apart from his marriage, he did not involve himself in any personal relationship that made emotional demands on him. His treatment of sex is cool and remarkably uncensorious. This is the way life is, he seems to be saying; this is how people behave, and whether we like or dislike it is not really relevant. Gabrielle is not a particularly complicated person, but one with a thwarted sex life which is largely responsible for her belief that she is the agency of the Dain curse of corruption. In *Red Harvest*, the relationship between Dinah Brand and Dan Rolff (a lunger like Hammett himself), to whom she is alternately affectionate and contemptuous, was one that the novelist perfectly understood.

To her (i.e. Nell Martin)

from him (i.e.

Dashiell Hammett)

February 20, 1930

Dashiell Hammett, ca. 1930 (Richard Layman)

With these two books published and a third on the way, Hammett felt ready to cut loose from the life he had been living, from the ties of family, even from San Francisco, which had been his home for eight years. He went first from the apartment on Post Street to one on Leavenworth Street, "an attractive, gable-windowed apartment house a few blocks west of the Mark Hopkins with an impressive view of downtown San Francisco."[32] There he lived with a woman named Nell Martin. The break cannot have come as a great surprise to Jose, who henceforth played little part in his life. The separation between them became complete when in October 1929 he and Nell Martin moved to New York. He had now finished *The Maltese Falcon* and knew, as he wrote to the Knopf editor, that this was the first fiction he had produced which was "the best [I] was capable of writing at the time [I] was writing it,"[33] strongly hinting that he could still do something better. He was not rich and indeed had to borrow $500 from the ever-amiable Albert Samuels to finance the move to New York, but he was deep into a fourth novel, which was to become *The Glass Key*, and his tuberculosis had been in remission for some time. He felt confidence in the future and assurance in the exercise of his talent. The good life was about to begin.

5

THE MALTESE FALCON

"IF this book had been written with the help of an outline or notes or even a clearly defined plot-idea in my head I might now be able to say how it came to be written and why it took the shape it did," Hammett wrote in the 1934 introduction to the Modern Library edition of *The Maltese Falcon,* which was honored by being the first crime story chosen for the series. No more than four years had elapsed since its publication, but he suggested with a lordly touch that he had forgotten these things, although he could remember where most of the characters had originated:

> Wilmer, the boy gun-man, was picked up in Stockton, California.... He was a neat small smooth-faced quiet boy of perhaps twenty-one.... He was serenely proud of the name the local newspapers gave him—The Midget Bandit.... Brigid O'Shaughnessy had two originals, one an artist, the other a woman who came to Pinkerton's San Francisco office to hire an operative to discharge her housekeeper, but neither of these women was a criminal....

Dundy's prototype I worked with in a North Carolina railroad yard; Cairo's I picked up on a forgery charge in Pasco, Washington, in 1920; Polhaus's was a former captain of detectives. . . . Gutman's was suspected—foolishly, as most people were—of being a German secret agent in Washington, D.C., in the early days of the war, and I never remember shadowing a man who bored me as much.[1]

There was no easy way of verifying such assertions, and their accuracy is less important than the way in which they show Hammett using that rich Pinkerton experience with the deliberate intention of impressing his audience. By the time he wrote the Modern Library introduction, *The Maltese Falcon* had been accepted as a classic. Indeed, it was greeted as such on publication. The writing was said to be better than Hemingway's; the book was called by Alexander Woollcott both "the best detective story America has yet produced" and an extremely well-written novel. Franklin P. Adams said that it was the first detective story he had read through to the end since the days of Sherlock Holmes.[2] *The Maltese Falcon* sold well, seven reprints being called for in the year of publication. It was published in Britain, and within twelve months film rights had been sold to Warner Brothers.

It was still by no means the best-seller of its year. Hammett's success as a writer (distinct from the money he was soon to earn from films) must be seen in perspective. Despite the high critical praise of *The Maltese Falcon*, the hard-boiled crime story remained something that many readers of mysteries found too violent and too crude for their taste. Van Dine faded from the scene during the thirties, but Ellery Queen flourished, and the small army of genteel women writers found a steady market. Hammett's books had no great success at this time in Britain or the rest of Europe. The hard-boiled story was an indigenous American species and for some years did not flourish elsewhere. Pulp in general remained badly paid, and writers moved out of it if they could, as Erle Stanley Gardner did after the publication of his first Perry Mason novel in 1933.

In his role as an occasional reviewer for the *Saturday Review of Literature* and later for the *New York Evening Post*, Hammett stressed the importance of realism and deplored the lack of it in the standard mystery story. Most of the books that came to him he called "carelessly manufactured improbabilities having more than their share of those blunders which

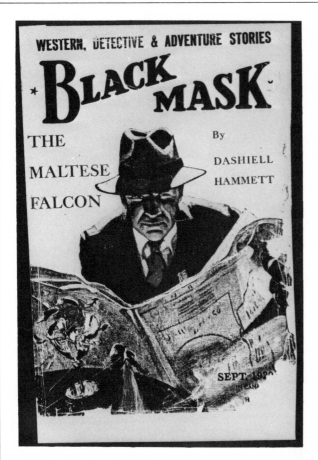

Part I of The Maltese Falcon *in* Black Mask,
September 1929 (UCLA)

The Maltese Falcon, *published by Knopf,
February 1930* (Richard Layman)

earn detective stories as a whole the sneers of the captious. . . . A fellow who takes detective stories seriously, I am annoyed by the stupid recurrence of these same blunders in book after book."[3] As always, he used the reviews to demonstrate his expertise, offering two dozen suggestions that "might be of value to somebody."[4] His remarks were strongly practical, although in some cases elementary, such as "a pistol, to be a revolver, must have something on it that revolves." Less obvious were technical pointers, for instance, that the effect of a silencer on the sound of a revolver shot is negligible or that a bullet from a Colt .45 usually knocks you over. This kind of knowledge was ignored by most detective story writers, who felt that such gross mechanical details would be out of place in their books, although something really unusual—say, a rare South American poison that could be added to soup instead of salt—might be worth describing in detail. The knowledge that a stab or shot sound is felt as a push at first and that you do not feel the blow that knocks you unconscious was a part of the world of a Pinkerton operative but not that of an English lady novelist at home among poisons and teacups. In one review Hammett did his best for his *Black Mask* colleague, friend, and drinking companion Raoul Whitfield, whose *Green Ice,* he said, offered "naked action pounded into tough compactness by staccato, hammerlike writing."[5] He may have been a little disconcerted when another reviewer said that Whitfield's book was the best detective story of the season. The reviews he wrote over a six-month period in 1930 for the *Post* must be among the most candid and unusual ever published. They earned little money but helped to confirm that he was more than a pulp writer, if confirmation was needed after *The Maltese Falcon.*

The differences between this and the two earlier novels are so great that they obviously reflect a long and serious effort to determine what had to be done if the crime story was to have a chance of being considered serious literature. The plots of the two first novels and the long short stories are extremely complicated, and in their violence and casualness, the way that people drift in and out of the action and minor figures do things of major importance, these works reflect the realities Hammett knew as a detective. In the *Falcon* he acknowledged for the first time that slices of raw life are one thing, artistic effectiveness another, and that a novel's form makes its own demands upon a writer. The plot here is quite straightforward. The telling gives a flavor of mystery, but we have no doubt from an early stage that a group of crooks, or perhaps more than one group, is searching for an immensely valuable figure in the form of a bird. The idea of the falcon came from Hammett's reading about the history of the Hospitalers of St. John, which strongly resembles the account given in the book, and includes the yearly gift of a falcon. This touch of authenticity to balance the romance of the crooks' quest for the bird is typical of Hammett. Before the resolution we are unsure of the role played by Brigid O'Shaughnessy, or at least readers at the time were unsure. The tradition that somebody loved by the hero must be a good woman was strong.

Along with the clear and credible plot goes a drastic reduction of violence. There are plenty of threats in the book, but all the serious violence takes place off-stage, such as the killing of Gutman. Hammett's denial that he had an outline, notes, or plot idea should be taken with a pinch of salt, for his avoidance of blazing and snapping guns—and of bullets kissing holes in doors or burning their woodwork—is a deliberate declaration that the days when every episode demanded its ration of violence and every ending its obligatory shoot-out are over. Out with the blazing guns goes the Op, in part because he cannot be contained within the new framework, in part, no doubt, because Hammett came to realize the limitations of a first-person narrative. The first person has the advantage of pace, lends itself to lively dialogue, and is ideal if for some reason the author particularly wants to show events from the perspective of one person. It means, however, that no action can be described, no motive assessed or speculation made, outside that individual's perceptions. Such a break would not have been made without careful thought, for almost all of Hammett's work had been written in the first person. It was a decisive step to replace the Op with Sam Spade.

The change meant more than putting in the place of an undersize and overweight figure one who was romantically interesting, with his V-shaped mouth and chin, yellow-gray eyes, and hair growing down to a point on his forehead, so that he looked "rather pleasantly like a blond satan."[6] Spade, said his creator in that Modern Library introduction, had no original and was consciously a fantasy. "He is a dream man in the sense that he is what most of the private detectives I worked with would like to have been and what quite a few of them in their cockier moments thought they approached . . . a hard and shifty fellow, able to take care of himself in any situation, able to get the best of anybody he comes in contact with, whether criminal, innocent by-stander or client." Implied was the thought that such a detective always had an eye on the main chance.

Today the name of Sam Spade has become synonymous with that of a tough hero, but one of the attractions in reading the book is our uncertainty about his honesty. There comes a point—perhaps for most readers near the end, in Chapter Nineteen, when Spade refuses to let Cairo walk out on Gutman, Brigid, and himself, saying irritably: "Good God! Is this the first thing you guys ever stole?"—when we are almost convinced that he is as crooked as the rest of them. Nor are these doubts dissipated when Brigid asks what he would have done if the falcon had been real, and he replies that it makes no difference now, adding: "A lot of money would have been at least one more item on the other side of the scales."[7] Spade's ethical code, never openly stated, is not identical with Op's. When a man's partner is killed, Spade says, something has to be done about it even though the partner is a stupid lecher like Miles Archer. But Spade adds this not as a matter of conscience, but because failure to find the killer would reflect badly on him. And in the brilliant "fall guy" chapter, with its undertone of vicious comedy, Spade's way of handling the police is to "toss them a victim, somebody they can hang the works on. . . . I never forget that when the day of reckoning comes I want to be all set to march into headquarters pushing a victim in front of me, saying: 'Here, you chumps, is your criminal.' "[8] We are never quite sure how nearly this is genuine and how much Spade is stringing the crooks along. The lasting ambiguity of the character makes Spade a much richer, more complex figure than Chandler's Marlowe or Ross Macdonald's Lew Archer.

The character was created to fit the new third-person approach, and the technique through which the story was told also differed from anything Hammett had used before. The opening characters are a series of dialogues, each between Spade and one other character and each taking the narrative one step further. Chapter One gives us Spade with Brigid as Miss Wonderly spinning a tale, and lets us know glancingly that Spade thinks little of his partner. In Chapter Two he talks to Detective Tom Polhaus, and the author drops the vital clue that the blast that killed Archer burned his coat. Next are Spade and Lieutenant Dundy: we learn that the detective skates often on the thinnest legal ice and that Dundy is waiting eagerly for the ice to break. Spade and Iva Archer: we find that he has been having an affair with his partner's wife. By this time we no longer regard Spade as a conventional detective hero, but it is still a shock when Iva asks, "Oh, Sam, did you kill him?" Spade and Miss Wonderly again: we discover that she is Brigid O'Shaughnessy and a congenital liar and that neither Spade nor Archer believed a word of her original story. "We believed your two hundred dollars."[9] At this point—and we are only halfway through Chapter Four—we have learned, very largely through dialogue and without a line of explicit comment from the author, a lot about Sam Spade. These opening chapters are a model in the art of developing a narrative and of revealing a character by indirection.

The person-to-person dialogues do not continue throughout the book, but character is rendered chiefly through dialogue, without much physical description. Casper Gutman is given a few excellent lines conveying his fatness, but his somehow old-fashioned and old-maidish menace is better represented by his black cutaway coat and vest, black satin Ascot tie, striped gray worsted trousers, and patent leather shoes. The best touch of all, however, is the elaborate falsity of his conversation, as when he gives a toast to plain speaking and clear understanding and expresses delight after Spade has said he likes to talk. "Better and better! I distrust a close-mouthed man. He generally picks the wrong time to talk and says the wrong things. . . . Now, sir, we'll talk if you like. And I'll tell you right out that I'm a man who likes talking to a man that likes to talk."[10] Joel Cairo is given us chiefly through his clothes, the flamboyant ruby in his cravat, the black derby in his chamois-gloved hand. The boy gunman, Wilmer Cook, is seen through his neat gray cap, his obscenity ("The boy spoke two words, the first a short guttural verb, the second, 'you' "),[11] and his lack of size, so that he looks like a schoolboy when confronted by Spade and a hotel detective. The two women with minor roles, Iva Archer and Spade's secretary, Effie Perine, are excellently defined through their relationship to the detective. Brigid, alone among the characters, has worn badly, in part because heroine-villains of this kind have become common in crime stories during recent years, in part because what seemed daring in 1930 ("Can I buy you with my body?"[12]) sounds hopelessly dated now.

Hammett's treatment of sex was, as usual, outspoken for the time. In crime stories of the period, whether genteel or rough, the hero did not bed his partner's wife, and it was unusual, although not unknown, for him to go to bed with a client. Spade sleeps with Brigid knowing that she is a crook, even suspecting that she is a murderer. In the morning he leaves her sleeping, examines her clothes, and then visits her apartment and searches it thoroughly, not merely looking in drawers and under rugs and furniture, but leaning out of windows, poking with a fork into powders and cream jars, examining food and food containers, emptying the garbage can, and draining the toilet tank so that he can check whether anything is hidden. (It is such meticulous attention to the facts of detective life that makes Spade a far more convincing figure than his rivals.) He does some shopping on the way back and arrives saying, "Young Spade bearing breakfast." At breakfast—business is business—he asks her about the black bird, and she says reproachfully, "You can't ask me to talk about that this morning of all mornings."[13]

That is not her only occasion for reproach. Later, when one $1,000 bill vanishes from the ten Gutman handed Spade (in fact, the fat man palmed it), the detective orders Brigid to strip in the bathroom to make sure she has not taken it and threatens that if she refuses, her clothes will be taken off in front of the others. And the finale, in which Spade says that "I'm going to send you over," tells her that he will wait for her, and adds that "if they hang you I'll always remember you," is the Op-and-Gabrielle scene from *The Dain Curse* played over again, but with significant differences. The Op was resisting the girl, whereas Spade has already taken her, and Gabrielle was innocent, whereas Brigid is guilty. Spade is, as his creator said, a hard and shifty fellow, and he prefers his own security to his love for Brigid. In the end she is the indispensable fall girl—although she can hardly be called that, because she is guilty—and Spade uses the Op's argument to the Princess in "The Gutting of Couffignal": "I'm a detective, and expecting me to run criminals down and then let them go free is like asking a dog to catch a rabbit and let it go."[14] This fine closing dialogue has the technical merit of avoiding the explanation at the end of a story that Hammett had sometimes handled rather awkwardly.

When he gave *The Maltese Falcon* to Knopf, Hammett asked that the publisher "go a little easy on the editing," saying that although he wouldn't go to the stake for his system of punctuation, "I do rather like it and I think it goes with my sort of sentence-structure."[15] Knopf's editor, Harry Block, wanted changes in what Hammett called the "to-bed and homosexual parts," but Hammett said he would like to leave them, since Block had also observed that they "would be all right perhaps in an ordinary novel."[16] There had already been trouble with Joseph Shaw when the story appeared in *Black Mask*. Brigid's line "I'm not ashamed to be naked before you" was deleted from the stripping scene, although it was reinstated in the book, and a line from Cairo to Brigid about "the one you couldn't make"[17] was also restored to the book after magazine censorship. On the other hand, a house detective's comment about Cairo was changed from "Oh, *her*!" in the magazine to the less explicit "Oh, that one."[18] The most comic of Shaw's objections was to a question Spade asks Wilmer: "How long have you been off the gooseberry lay, son?" Shaw thought it had homosexual implications, when in fact it was slang for stealing things from a clothesline.[19] "Gooseberry," deleted from the magazine, was returned to the book, but "gunsel" got through in both, in the belief that it was slang for a gunman, whereas in fact, along with "gazooney" and "bronc," it meant a kept boy.[20]

Some incidents in the book had their origin in other stories. In the Modern Library introduction "The Whosis Kid" and "The Gutting of Couffignal" are mentioned, but such resemblances tend to be particular rather than general, like the Op's treatment of the Princess. In an otherwise undistinguished early story, "Who Killed Bob Teal," the murder of Teal, a young detective, was identical with Archer's murder by Brigid. The gun was held close enough to singe Teal's coat, and the Op explains at the end that the question in the story's title can have only one answer. "Bob wasn't a boob!... He wouldn't have died with empty hands, from a gun that was close enough to scorch his coat. The murderer *had* to be somebody Bob trusted"—in other words, his client.[21] In the novel Spade tells Brigid that Miles didn't have many brains but would never have been caught in a blind alley with his gun tucked away on his hip and his overcoat buttoned. "You were his client... and if you caught up with him and asked him to go up there he'd've gone. He was just dumb enough for that."[22]

The actual writing in *The Maltese Falcon* shows the author's determination to move out of the pulp world into that of the genuine novelist. It is not only the guns pumping lead that have gone. Slang is used less liberally, and attention is paid to the need for continuity and to the development of character. In the lectures on the mystery story that he gave years later in New York, Hammett stressed, as one student remembered, "that tempo is the vital thing in fiction, that you've got to keep things moving,

Hammett's San Francisco, late 1920s (San Francisco Public Library)

Market Street at Powell

Geary Street from Grant Avenue

Hotel St. Francis lobby (St. Mark in The Maltese Falcon)

Hotel Bellevue cafe (Belvedere in The Maltese Falcon)

and that character can be drawn *within* the action."[23] It was such drawing of character within the action, including action within the dialogue, that Hammett achieved here and in later novels to a degree approached among his contemporaries only by Hemingway. The good, hard phrases found in the earlier work were not sacrificed. Typical of them are the lawyer Sid Wise's remark, "You don't cash many checks for strangers, do you, Sammy?"[24] and Spade's caustic observation to Gutman after he has disarmed Wilmer and given Wilmer's pistols to the fat man, "A crippled newsie took them away from him, but I made him give them back."[25] It is true that the style has its limitations, or rather, that there are some clichés of the pulp story that Hammett never discarded. Spade does too much "wolfish grinning," and his eyes are "hard and cold," "narrow and sultry," "wary and dull," "angry," "bulging," "brooding"—all within a few pages.[26]

The book's effectiveness rests in part in the realization, fuller and richer than in the short stories, of San Francisco's streets and scenes. Spade waits for Cairo outside the Geary Theater on Sutter Street, sits with Effie Perine in Julius's Castle on Telegraph Hill, has an apartment on Post Street. Joe Gores, author of the novel *Hammett*, has traced many of the places exactly, for instance identifying Brigid's room at "the Coronet on California Street" as the Yerba Buena Apartments on Sutter Street.

There remains the question of symbolism. The falcon itself is often seen by critics as symbolic, because what should be a jeweled bird proves to be no more than black enamel coating lead. It is "a suitable symbol for illusory wealth" in "a novel about the destructive power of greed," Richard Layman says, and William F. Nolan thinks that "the falcon is a symbol for the falseness and illusions of life itself." Ross Macdonald suggested that the falcon might symbolize the lost cultures of the Mediterranean past "which have become inaccessible to Spade and his generation," or might even stand for the Holy Ghost itself. The absence of spiritual beliefs in Spade, he wrote, "seem[s] to me to make his story tragedy, if there is such a thing as dead-pan tragedy."[27] This surely goes much too far. Almost any crime story can be said to express the destructive power of something or other, whether it be greed, sex, hatred, or envy. We are all aware of the deadliness of the Seven Deadly Sins. And although it may be that a true awareness of past, or indeed present, culture is absent in a man like Sam Spade, his solution can surely be called tragic only if Spade, even momentarily, suffers tragically. But the detective's emotional struggle is merely between the romantic feeling of his love for Brigid and the practical need to offer the police a murderer, and there is no doubt that the practical approach is going to win. One can read symbols into anything, but there is no indication that the falcon was chosen for any reason other than to provide a good focal point for a thriller, a focal point which also had a basis in fact.

There is more reason for attributing symbolism to the Flitcraft story, told by Spade to Brigid as one of his detective experiences. Flitcraft is a Tacoma real estate executive who has a pleasant house, a new car, and "the rest of the appurtenances of successful American living," including a wife and two sons. He goes out to lunch one day and never comes back. Spade finds Flitcraft five years later, living in the Northwest with another wife, and a baby son—the same kind of woman and the same kind of life. What had happened to him? On the way out to lunch Flitcraft was almost hit by a beam falling from an office building in course of construction. The near escape from injury and possible death showed him that the life he was living, "a clean, orderly, sane, responsible affair," was really a foolish one. "Life could be ended for him at random by a falling beam: he would change his life at random by simply going away." So he leaves, but after a couple of years he duplicates his previous existence. "That's the part of it I always liked," Spade says. "He adjusted himself to beams falling, and then no more of them fell, and he adjusted himself to them not falling."

The Flitcraft story is extremely well told. It has nothing to do with the plot, but we, like Brigid, find it absorbingly interesting. The records of any police department will confirm that its basic elements are not unusual. Apparently happy husbands or wives often disappear from their pleasant homes to lead a new life, generally with another woman or man but sometimes for no obvious logical reason. In fiction Georges Simenon has played several variations on the theme, as in *The Man Who Watched the Trains Go By*, in which Kees Popinga suddenly realizes that the pattern of his respectable life is a fraud, abandons his wife and family, becomes a multiple murderer, and ends up in an asylum. There he starts to write an article, "The Truth about the Kees Popinga Case," but fails to complete it because, as he says to his doctor, "Really, there isn't any truth about it, is there?" Undoubtedly Hammett meant something by inserting this enigmatic story into a tale to which it bears no obvious relation, but what?

Most of the interpretations are based on the falling beam and what it made Flitcraft understand about the universe. "The randomness of the universe is Spade's vision throughout," says Robert I. Edenbaum.[28] Layman points out that the nineteenth-century American philosopher Charles Sanders Pierce (Flitcraft changes his name to Charles Pierce) wrote about random occurrence.[29] John Cawelti suggests that Hammett's vision is of an irrational cosmos in which all the rules can be overturned in a moment,[30] and William Ruehlmann that the tale is meant to show that Spade, like Flitcraft, is incapable of emotional involvement and so is truly committed to nobody. All the characters in the book, according to this view, are counterfeits: Brigid a counterfeit innocent, Gutman a counterfeit sage, Wilmer a counterfeit tough guy. "Worst of all is Spade, a counterfeit hero."[31] George J. Thompson, one of the most intelligent critics of Hammett's work, says that "the meaning of the Flitcraft parable is that if we can see clearly enough to understand that external reality is unstable and unpredictable, then one must be ready to react to its ironies. . . . To some extent the Flitcraft parable, like the Maltese falcon, stands for the absurdity of assuming that the external world is necessarily stable."[32]

There are other theories, all based on Hammett's belief in the random nature of life. Without expressing positive disagreement with any of them, it should perhaps be added that with Hammett the most straightforward, least high-flown view of the Flitcraft story is likely to be the one he had in mind. It is possible that he was not contemplating a grand application of the story to all human existence but merely a personal reference to his own career to date. In that case the key sentence is "What disturbed him was the discovery that in sensibly ordering his affairs he had got out of step, and not into step, with life." Up to the time of his departure from San Francisco, Hammett had done his best to order his life sensibly, without much success. For several years afterward, however, he made no attempt to order it at all.

Whether or not this idea has any validity, those prone to fine-spun theories about Flitcraft in particular and Hammett's work in general should remember his response to Lillian Hellman on an occasion when he had killed a snapping turtle, first by rifle shot and then by an ax blow almost severing the head, only to find that the dead turtle had moved down the garden in the night. When Hammett started to cut away one leg from the shell, the other leg moved. Was the turtle alive or dead? Hellman rang the New York Zoological Society and was told that it was scientifically dead but that the society was not equipped to give a theological opinion.

"Then how does one define life?" Hellman asked Hammett.

"Lilly, I'm too old for that stuff," he replied.[33]

He would always have been too old for some of the theories put forward about the meaning of Flitcraft.

6

THE GOOD
LIFE BEGINS

THE affair between Hammett and Nell Martin did not last long, and his behavior during these first months in New York suggests that he sensed one way of life ending, and another beginning. *The Maltese Falcon* appeared between covers in February 1930, and in the following month *The Glass Key* began to appear in *Black Mask*, serialized in four installments like the earlier novels. During the same year two Op stories appeared in the magazine, "Death and Company" and "The Farewell Murder." They are among the better short stories, with a particularly fine description in the latter of a character named Captain Sherry, but they are still much inferior to the novels. These were the final Op stories and the last things he wrote for *Black Mask*, in spite of frequent pleas from Joseph Shaw, one of them accompanied by a check. The fact that bigger checks were offered elsewhere was no doubt important, but basically Hammett stopped writing pulp fiction because he believed he could do better. He was still working hard, writing a novel a year plus several short stories, occasional articles, and book reviews, but he found time to do a good deal of drinking, with Raoul Whitfield and another *Black Mask* contributor named Frederick Nebel, among others.

More than a year earlier Hammett had hoped he was about to break into Hollywood by the sale of some Op stories for filming, but the deal had fallen through. Whether consciously or not, he was waiting for another call, and in July 1930 it came. The movie rights to *Red Harvest* had been bought by Paramount, and a film was made called *Roadhouse Nights*, which contained little of the book's plot and none of its feeling. In June *The Maltese Falcon* was bought, to be made into a film with Ricardo Cortez as Spade, Bebe Daniels miscast as Brigid (called only Ruth Wonderly in the film), and Dudley Digges excellent as Gutman. Just after the book had been bought, David O. Selznick, then an executive at Paramount, told his boss, B. P. Schulberg, that they had a chance to secure Hammett, who was, Selznick said, "another Van Dine." The comparison is proof only of Van Dine's popularity—a number of his books were made into films—for Selznick must have known Hammett was nothing like Van Dine as a writer. Selznick said Hammett was "unspoiled as to money" and suggested engaging him on a contract for four weeks at $300 a week, with an option of eight further weeks at the same figure, plus a $5,000 bonus for an original story accepted for production.[1] To realize what such a contract was worth to Hammett, it should be noted that he got an advance of only $1,000 for *The Maltese Falcon*.

The young Gary Cooper was the rising star in the Paramount firmament, and Hammett was told that the studio wanted a gangster film with class for Cooper. He produced a story line over a weekend and then expanded it into an outline. Although a good deal of adaptation was needed, the story was produced as *City Streets*, with Cooper and the almost unknown Sylvia Sidney.

The experience should have been instructive for Hammett. His talents were just what Hollywood producers needed. He was full of ideas, was skilled at writing lively, naturalistic dialogue, and had a strong sense of drama. But although Hammett was useful to Hollywood, Hollywood could do nothing but damage to Hammett as a writer. It was prepared to use the talent but rejected the feeling behind it. The brutality of the stories, the unheroic quality of the men, and the shopworn nature of the women were entirely unacceptable to a Hollywood ruled by the Hays code, a

Hammett at the height of his literary career, ca. 1930 (UTA)

world where the monster moguls sincerely believed as they lined their pockets that they had a duty to show an America where all heroes were based on Sir Galahad, and if women erred it was only in the way Guinevere had in her love for Lancelot. This Hollywood did not last forever (not much more than a decade later Raymond Chandler was able to script James M. Cain's *Double Indemnity* with some faithfulness to the sordid quality of the original) but it was the one which prevailed in the thirties. It was typical of the Hollywood moral code of the day that Sylvia Sidney should play a girl who rejected her crooked past and tried to go straight and that Cooper should have come to her aid when she was framed for murder. Women crooks in Hammett's stories were simply crooked, and when Hammett saw the completed film, the only thing he liked was Sylvia Sidney's performance.

City Streets was his sole screen credit for Paramount, although he worked on other scripts. But it was only the beginning of his Hollywood life. He was put under contract by Darryl F. Zanuck at Warner Brothers to write an original Sam Spade story, starring William Powell, for a fee of $15,000 to be paid in three installments. (The esteem in which he was held can be gauged by the fact that when Chandler was put under contract to collaborate with Billy Wilder in scripting *Double Indemnity*, he was paid $750 a week.) The script was Hammett's second attempt to write something serious for the movies, and its fate marked the end of his interest in the cinema except as a means of making money. The film was to be about a Spade who was not simply a hard and shifty fellow but actually crooked. A news item of the time was headed "New Film to Expose Private Sleuth Racket," and this was the story that Hammett wrote. When Zanuck considered the story, however, he turned it down and refused to pay the last installment of the money. Three years later the basic idea was sold to Universal, with Spade (renamed Gene Richmond) identified as a cheat and blackmailer, a man who swindles and admits cheerfully: 'Sure, I'm always on the make." By the time this idea reached the screen, however, with Richmond's name changed to T. N. Thompson so that the film could be called *Mister Dynamite* from his initials, it had turned into a light comedy containing plenty of murders, with Edmund Lowe in the title role. The gap between conception and execution might have been enough to disillusion anybody.

It is possible, however, that Hammett never had any illusions about

The first film treatment of The Maltese
Falcon, *Warner Bros., 1931; from left:
Ricardo Cortez as Spade, J. Farrell
McDonald, Bebe Daniels as Brigid/Ruth
Wonderly, and Robert Elliott*

City Streets, *Paramount, 1931, with Gary
Cooper and a virtually unknown Sylvia
Sidney*

Hollywood. The life he lived there, almost from the beginning, was one of hard drinking, casual spending, and womanizing. He found no difficulty, then and after, in attracting women, many of whom admired the aloofness that marked his behavior when sober and perhaps enjoyed his total recklessness when drunk. He drank with other screenwriters who had come to Hollywood to make their fortune, with film starlets whom he later took to bed, and with total strangers. Ben Hecht, an avant-garde writer of the early twenties who had settled for Hollywood money, remembered parties at which Hammett and Hecht's collaborator Charles MacArthur took the drinking lead early in the evening and held on to it without sign of strain. Drinking was often combined with gambling, at which Hammett was not conspicuously successful. He hired a black chauffeur and servant named Jones, who drove him from Los Angeles to San Francisco so that he could pay back in person the $500 loan from Albert Samuels. The repayment was succeeded by a week-long party at one of the city's best hotels. When it was over, Hammett had to borrow more money from Samuels to finance the trip back. He sent a note to Samuels' bookkeeper, carried by the black chauffeur: "Give the jig the money. Dashiell Hammett."[2]

At this time he met Lillian Hellman, by far the most important woman in his life, as he was the most important man in hers. She described the meeting years afterward: "We met when I was twenty-four years old and he was thirty-six in a restaurant in Hollywood. The five-day drunk had left the wonderful face looking rumpled, and the very tall thin figure was tired and sagged. We talked of T. S. Eliot, although I no longer remember what we said, and then went and sat in his car and talked at each other and over each other until it was daylight."[3]

Hellman has written at various times a good deal about their relationship. The portrait she draws is somewhat sentimentalized and erratic in detail. Dates are occasionally wrong, incidents didn't occur quite in the way she describes them, and perhaps some of them didn't happen at all. "The memories skip about and make no pattern and I know only certain of them are to be trusted."[4] Yet even if one is skeptical of many Hellman-Hammett stories, there is no doubt that she is the most vital single witness to his character and behavior. The daughter of German-Jewish parents, she was brought up in New Orleans (described in her memoir *An Unfinished Woman*), and from the time she left college was intent on a literary career. When she met Hammett she was married to the Jewish humorous writer Arthur Kober, who was working for Paramount. In the early thirties they separated, without ill feeling, as she put it, and were divorced. Hammett also remained friendly with Kober. Hellman never remarried.

Each held compelling attractions for the other. For Hellman he was and remained a marvelously attractive man. Later in their relationship, after he had been ill, she saw him on a dockside, "the white hair, the white pants, the white shirt," and thought, "Maybe that's the handsomest sight I ever saw, that line of a man, the knife for a nose."[5] The recklessness of his behavior—the money slipping through his hands like mercury, some of it given away to any stranger who asked for it, the gambling, the drinking— all this seemed to the young woman the way life should be lived. In particular, she was happy at this time to match him drink for drink during an evening. She admired him as a writer, and the fact that he was so widely courted in Hollywood and elsewhere did not lessen her admiration. As the years went by she became less concerned with the glamor and more respectful of the dignity with which he bore himself in any situation, except on those occasions when he passed out dead drunk.

The attractions she held for Hammett were various, and they only began with her physical vitality, lively and flexible voice, flair for wearing clothes, and capacity for drink. As a self-educated man he was distrustful of intellectual women, but here was one much younger than himself, with respectable intellectual credentials, who still left him feeling at ease when they were talking about Eliot or Joyce. Her extroverted nature and quick enthusiasm, the bursts of temper easily forgotten, delighted one whose character was introverted, whose reactions were instantly skeptical. Hellman once told a friend Hammett had said "all he had ever wanted in the world was a docile woman but, instead, had come out with me."[6] Yet he did not really want a docile woman but one who, like Hellman, would call him when they were parted, ask, "Is there a lady in my bedroom?" and accept his answer, "I don't think so, but they come and go."[7] On another occasion she called him from New York at 3:00 in the morning, was told by the woman who answered that she was Hammett's secretary, and knowing that he had no secretary, flew out to Los Angeles drinking heavily on the plane, smashed the grandiose soda fountain in the house Hammett had rented from Harold Lloyd, and flew back to New York.[8] Whether or not this tale is accurate in every detail, the conduct was typical of Hellman and was something he enjoyed. In spite of these tantrums she was entirely

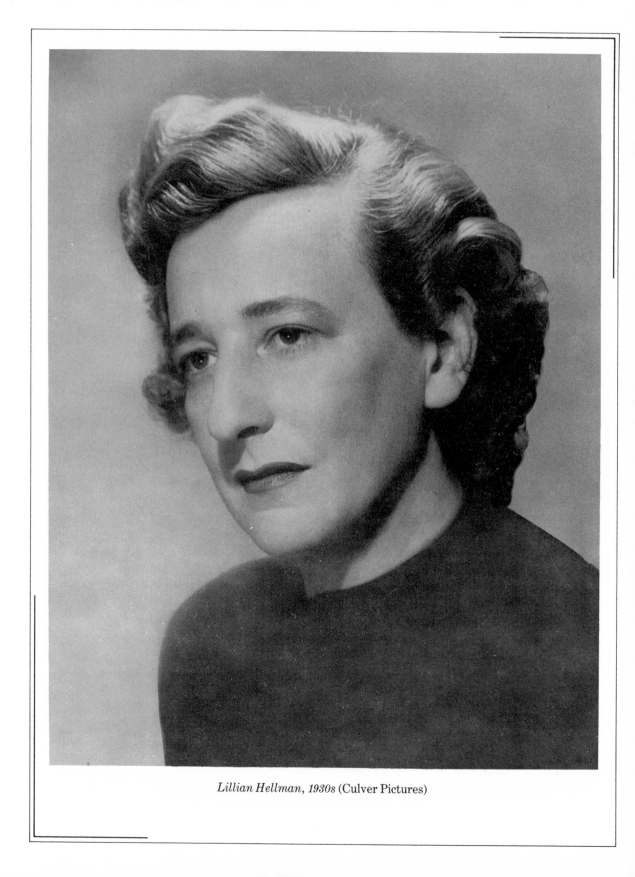

Lillian Hellman, 1930s (Culver Pictures)

tolerant of his sleeping around, which was what she understood him to mean when he said that because of her absence "I have to go on practically masturbating." He was similarly tolerant when he had bad reports of her behavior in the East, saying merely: "Ts! Ts! Ts! Just a she-Hammett."[9]

He found in Hellman an independence as proud and emphatic as his own. She lived with him periodically, but neither of them seems to have contemplated marriage. She had published only a few short stories when they met and was working at the poorly paid job of scenario reader, so their relationship as writers was at the beginning more or less that of teacher and student. But she relinquished none of her individuality. It was apparently Hammett who brought to her attention a true story set in Scotland about a girls' school forced to close because of rumors that the owners were lesbians. This became the basis of her first produced play, *The Children's Hour*, the published version of which was dedicated to Hammett. The play was produced in 1934, the year in which his career as a writer effectively ended. The way their positions as celebrated writers would change is curiously foreshadowed in a short story he published in 1932, in which a Hollywood screenwriter loses his job at the same time that his girl friend gets her first serious screen part. In a sentimental stiff-upper-lip ending, he refuses her offer to marry him and goes away so that he will not be a drag on her career. The story is called "On the Way."[10]

Hammett's highly promiscuous sex life did not go untroubled. He got a second and very bad dose of gonorrhea, which landed him in the hospital. The treatment was extremely painful, the recovery slow. After he was better, he became involved in a court case in which a starlet charged that he had invited her to his Hollywood hotel room for dinner and there beat and tried to rape her. He made no appearance at the trial, and she was awarded $2,500 in damages instead of the $35,000 for which she had asked. The affair had no effect on his reputation, which had reached its peak with the book publication in 1931 of *The Glass Key*.

7

THE GLASS KEY

T H E R E is general agreement that *The Maltese Falcon* and *The Glass Key* are Hammett's two finest books. With the passing years he looked more and more harshly on his own fiction, but he conceded that *The Glass Key* was "not so bad."[1] Its reception was even better than that of the previous novel, and so were the sales, 20,000 copies having been sold eighteen months after publication. Some critics preferred the *Falcon*, others said simply that Hammett had written the three best detective stories of all time, and in the *New Yorker* Dorothy Parker screamed that "there is entirely too little screaming about the work of Dashiell Hammett."[2] She continued in the same vein when, on meeting him, she fell to her knees and kissed his hand, an act that, according to Hellman, earned her his lasting dislike.

 The Glass Key, like *The Maltese Falcon,* is written in the third person, with the effect, no doubt intended, of creating a sense of detachment from the characters. Although it is in a formal sense a murder mystery, it is

basically a novel about politics and the use of power. Paul Madvig is a political boss in an unnamed city, evidently much bigger than Personville. It is election year, and he should be concerned with getting his candidates elected by the usual means of bribery and coercion. Madvig, however, has fallen for Janet Henry, daughter of a senator who is standing for reelection. Without Madvig's support Henry has no chance, but by backing him the boss is alienating many of his supporters and damaging his own position. Madvig's self-interest is at war with his desire to move up the social scale —or, if one likes to put it differently, with his love for Janet Henry.

It is possible, T. S. Eliot said, to write a play on two levels, one providing drama and excitement for the groundlings, the other saying something of deeper interest for those able to apprehend it. The comic scenes in Shakespeare's tragedies and histories are there for the audience's amusement, and *Macbeth* was for many people in Shakespeare's time and today a blood-and-thunder melodrama. Even Eliot's own *Murder in the Cathedral* can be seen as a tale of conspiracy ending in murder rather than as a study of idealism and pride. In the same way, *The Glass Key* can be, and often is, read as an excellent mystery story and nothing more. On this level the book's subject is: Who killed the senator's son, Taylor Henry? Because Madvig is suspected, his trusted right-hand man, Ned Beaumont, sets out to solve the crime and thus clear his boss. As Hammett said, the clues to the murder are nicely placed, although he was right to add that few people seemed to have noticed this fact. The stick and the hat are as good as any such clues in Agatha Christie.

The puzzle is undoubtedly part of the enjoyment of the tale, but to read it solely for the mystery is to oversimplify a story with many ramifications. Beaumont is not only Madvig's henchman but also his friend, subtle where Madvig is direct, intelligent and perceptive where the political boss is crude and ignorant. The story is partly about masculine friendship, about the risks and beatings Beaumont will take in his attempt to protect his friend and the strain placed on their relationship when both men fall in love with Janet Henry. Yet Beaumont is even less of a hero than Sam Spade. William F. Nolan calls him an outright crook; another critic, Peter Wolfe, says he has sold out to the political machine. According to Wolfe, he is "a believer in the spoils system, [who] hands out bribes, sinecures, and patronage jobs in return for political favors."[3] Such comments seem far too strong. In appearance and style, Beaumont resembles his creator. He is clear-eyed, erect, and tall, with a flat chest that suggests constitutional weakness. He knows that you don't wear brown shoes with a blue suit or silk socks with tweeds. We are told nothing about his background except that he has come from New York. He is shown to us as a compulsive gambler (like Hammett), a political manipulator in Madvig's service, but above all a man whose loyalty to his friend is unswerving until Janet Henry appears. This potentially corny theme is handled with remarkable delicacy.

The early chapters again take the form of dialogues, which give us the outline of the plot and show us the characters almost entirely through indirection. The brief sections of the opening chapter provide a great deal of information through conversation without for a moment impeding the narrative flow. Section One tells us in a single page that Beaumont is a gambler on an unlucky streak and that he is the henchman of a political boss. Section Two, Beaumont-Madvig, lays out the political situation in detail. Madvig's lack of social skills is shown very clearly in his resentment at being told that he should give Janet Henry nothing for her birthday. When he says he is going to marry her, Beaumont advises him: "Make them put it in writing and swear to it before a notary and post a cash bond, or, better still, insist on the wedding before election day."[4] We finish this section knowing that Madvig is in real political trouble and is trusting Beaumont to keep his own supporters in order. We know also, as they calmly talk about the right time to square a case against a Madvig man in jail on a hit-and-run manslaughter charge, that they are both unscrupulous men. Section Three shows Beaumont stalling about the manslaughter case. In Section Four he learns that he has won $3,000 on a racing bet, he finds Taylor Henry's body—and we get the first hint that Madvig may be a suspect. Section Five tells us that Beaumont is dissatisfied with the newspaper story of the murder, and sections Six and Seven, that the bookmaker who took his bet has left town, leaving behind Taylor Henry's IOUs. Section Eight gives us Madvig at home with his mother and shows us Beaumont as a gambler with a total belief in luck. "What good am I if my luck's gone? Then I cop, or think I do, and I'm right again."[5] In the final section Beaumont talks to Madvig's daughter Opal and persuades her to get him one of the dead man's hats. Later he uses the hat in a brilliantly ingenious—and again unscrupulous—trick to make the bookmaker pay up.

This whole opening chapter takes no more than twenty pages. It is a masterpiece of compressed storytelling. In particular, it tells us all that we need to know about Madvig and Beaumont and their relationship. It is no surprise to learn that they are happy to stay on good terms with the city's gangsters, the object on both sides being to run a peaceful city in which the gangsters get rich and are prepared to pay the politicians to leave them alone. Shad O'Rory, the gang leader, bribes the cops, and the cops do what Madvig tells them. But Madvig's support of Senator Henry affects this peaceful coexistence. When Madvig closes down some of Shad's dives in the name of Prohibition enforcement, the gangster protests: "Business is business and politics is politics. Let's keep them apart." And when Madvig refuses, he warns, "It's going to mean killing."[6] Madvig's action does not, of course, spring from civic feeling. He is slapping the gangster down because Shad is making trouble for him politically, and rejects Beaumont's advice that closing the dives is "like using a cyclone shot to blow off a safe-door when you could get it off without any fuss by using a come-along."[7]

Again like *The Maltese Falcon, The Glass Key* contains no onstage murders, and no guns blaze. The city is as corrupt as Personville, but Beaumont's methods are not the Op's but those of a gambler prepared to bet his own life and safety in his master's service. When Janet Henry says he is a gentleman, he corrects her: "I'm a gambler and a politician's hanger-on." At the end of the same scene, knowing that she suspects Madvig of having killed her brother, he tells her: "You're right about my being Paul's friend. I'm that no matter who he killed."[8] This kind of loyalty leads to the most extraordinary scenes in the book, those in which Beaumont deliberately places himself in the hands of Shad's minions. The detailed account of Beaumont's beating at the hands of Shad's humorously sadistic thug Jeff was the first of its kind in fiction and remains among the most effective. Most beatings are no more convincing in print than they are on the screen, but the several pages in which Beaumont is slapped down time and again by the moronic Jeff are of a different kind. As he staggers toward the door and manages to reach it, Jeff says genially, "Now there, Houdini," and drives his fist into Beaumont's face so that he slides again to the floor.[9] When Shad wants to speak to him, Beaumont is revived by a cold-water soaking and slaps from Jeff. Later, as Beaumont tries again and again to get out of the room where he is being kept, Jeff punches him unconscious each time and says: "I never seen a guy that liked being hit so much or that I liked hitting so much."[10] In the end Beaumont escapes by starting a fire in the room and letting himself drop from a window.

More remarkable still is a later scene in which Beaumont again deliberately puts himself into Jeff's power. The thug is astonished and delighted to see him. "He's a—a God-damned massacrist, that's what he is," Jeff says, adding that the small room above the bar where they are drinking is just the place for them. "I can bounce you around off the walls. That way we won't be wasting a lot of time while you're getting up off the floor."[11] This vein of graveyard humor runs through Hammett's writing but is exploited most successfully here, right on to the end, when Jeff is needled into strangling Shad while Beaumont looks on without attempting to interfere.

Hammett said in an interview years later that he wrote the last third of the book in one continuous thirty-hour writing session.[12] If this is true, it may explain some of the questions that the reader is left asking. One is surprised that, although Madvig lives with his mother and daughter, no wife is ever mentioned, dead or divorced. And we often wonder about the exact purpose of Ned Beaumont's behavior. In Chapter Six he deliberately flirts with and embraces Mrs. Mathews, wife of a newspaper publisher, so that her husband will be upset. The distraught Mathews shoots himself, but that can hardly have been Beaumont's intention. Was he simply out to cause trouble, or did he have a more positive purpose? In Chapter Nine Shad is killed by Jeff, but again this was not calculable in advance. If it had not happened, how would Beaumont's visit have helped Madvig? Probably the general answer to such questions is that Beaumont deliberately stirred up trouble, gambling that at the end he would come out on top. In this book Hammett again indulged much too freely his weakness for describing eyes. On two consecutive pages various eyes are "shiny with merriment . . . glassy and dreadful . . . like blue-gray ice . . . stricken . . . cool, deliberate."[13] And the catalog could be greatly extended.

Yet such minor flaws do not seriously affect the book's originality nor its quality as a view of one kind of American life at the time. Its technique of revealing character by indirection was pushed much further by Hammett than by Hemingway and was not attempted by any other American novelist between the wars. In Hemingway's *The Sun Also Rises* and *A*

Farewell to Arms characterization is confined to the central figures, and we understand little about such important characters as Robert Cohn and Bill Gorton. In *The Glass Key* everything is shown by indirection. We learn so much about Beaumont's personality through his brief visit to New York, the shady figures he knows there, and his night with the girl he calls Fednik, that we do not need to be told anything of his background. Narration of this kind is on a high level of art. And, to move from major to minor characters, we learn from Beaumont's conversations with Opal Madvig everything necessary about her relationship to her father. The action of the "Observer" chapter conveys perfectly the emotional gap that yawns between Mathews and his wife, Eloise. We read this chapter with equal admiration for its plotting skills and for the icy accuracy with which these very minor figures are delineated; both the wife's philandering with Beaumont and the husband's suicide seem perfectly logical (although, as has already been said, Beaumont's awareness of this as a likely outcome does not). Another of the book's strengths as a novel is that it allows no easy consolations. The election at its core is no conventional conflict between clean and dirty government. When Beaumont tells Madvig that everybody in town thinks he killed Taylor Henry and that one of his ward bosses has changed allegiance because he figures they are going to lose, Madvig asks: "He figures they'd rather have Shad running the city than me? He figures being suspected of one murder makes my rep worse than Shad's?"[14] And this is the realistic choice: either Shad, the well-dressed gangster, or Madvig, the machine politician who rests on bribery and patronage. In the end Madvig deliberately hands over the city's government to Shad's lieutenants while he builds a new organization, and Beaumont agrees that "it's the best way to play it."[15] In such a world there is no place for idealism.

The book makes a deliberate use of symbolism. The title is based on a dream of Janet Henry's, in which she and Beaumont are lost in a forest and come to a house in which they see a table piled high with food, but with hundreds of snakes slithering about the floor. They climb onto the roof, he leans down and unlocks the door, the snakes come out, and "we jumped down and ran inside and locked the door and ate and ate and ate."[16] That is the dream as she tells it at first. In the last chapter, however, after she has agreed to go with Beaumont to New York, she tells him the dream's true end. "The key was glass and shattered in our hands just as we got the door open. . . . We couldn't lock the snakes in and they came out all over us and I woke up screaming."[17]

Commentators have had a field day with Janet's nightmare, from suggestions that it implies Beaumont's sexual impotence (the only basis for this idea is that he beds nobody in the book)[18] or Janet's sexual guilt and incestuous feelings toward her father (which have equally little foundation), to the view that the key opens a kind of Pandora's box of troubles or even that Beaumont himself is the glass key, "fragile in character and, at the end, broken."[19] The attraction of symbolic interpretations is that they can never be disproved. But here there seems no reason to go much beyond a perhaps disappointing commonsense view, that the glass key is meant to symbolize only that the relationship between Beaumont and Janet will not last. Perhaps it suggests also by extension that each of us is alone with his or her box of horrors and that any easy attempt to get rid of them is bound to fail. Hammett's own view of sexual relationships, and of any permanent link between a man and a woman, was not optimistic. *The Maltese Falcon* was dedicated to Jose and *The Glass Key* to Nell Martin, and in both cases the dedication was a kind of signing-off thank-you, for he had parted from both women before the books dedicated to them were published.

8

THE THIN MAN

BACK in New York and now employing two agents, one for films and the other for books, Hammett enjoyed himself. Hellman is not explicit about how much they lived together, but she presumably shared his apartment on East 38th Street when she was in New York, and in her absence it was inhabited by others. He complained a few years later that it was easy to be bored making the same round of New York clubs every night, seeing the same faces at parties and hearing the same lies, but in the early thirties he was less blasé. He was most at ease with hard drinkers like himself and got on very well with William Faulkner when the southern writer paid a visit to New York. They did not agree about the merits of Thomas Mann's *The Magic Mountain*, which Faulkner greatly admired and Hammett said gave a false impression of the atmosphere in a home or clinic for the tubercular. Hammett refused to accept Faulkner's assertion that *Sanctuary* was a potboiler, saying that no true writer ever set out deliberately just to write a potboiler. (Some defensiveness about much of his own work was obviously involved.) They met happily, however, as devoted drinkers, particularly of whiskey.

Among the more outrageous episodes during Faulkner's stay was one that began when they met the publisher Bennett Cerf for lunch. On learning that Cerf was going to the Knopfs' for dinner that evening, Hammett insisted that he and Faulkner should go along, since Blanche Knopf would certainly wish to meet Faulkner. Cerf's heart must have sunk when they said they would stay in the bar and wait to be collected, especially since it was a black-tie dinner party, but Hammett was not to be denied. They were duly collected, still improperly dressed for the evening, and were delivered to the dinner party almost blind drunk. Hammett managed to effect the introduction of Faulkner to Blanche Knopf and then sank to the carpet. Faulkner moved to help him and collapsed by his side. Both men had to be taken back to their hotels.[1] It may have been at this time that the Knopfs began to feel that they were paying a heavy price for having Dashiell Hammett on their list.

All this was agreeable play for a man who called himself in an interview a two-fisted loafer able to "loaf longer and better than anybody I know," adding that his hobbies were drinking and playing poker.[2] But what about writing? His literary agent, Ben Wasson, was keen to have something, anything, of Hammett's to sell. In the year that *The Glass Key* was published in volume form, there were no short stories, but Hammett gave Wasson a sizable piece (nearly twenty thousand words) of a new book, to be called *The Thin Man*. When the typescript of this never-completed work was auctioned more than a decade later, Hammett provided an explanatory note saying that "by the time I had written these 65 pages my publisher and I agreed that it might be wise to postpone the publication of 'The Glass Key'—scheduled for that fall—until the following spring. So—having plenty of time—I put these 65 pages aside and went to Hollywood for a year." Later, he went on, he found it easier to use only the basic idea of the plot, so that in terms of a novel, "except for . . . the use of the characters' names Guild and Wynant—this unfinished manuscript has a clear claim to virginity."[3]

There are some unlikely points in this explanation of the book's abandonment. The dating is a little uncertain, for although Hammett may have written it in 1930, Wasson did not offer the extract until the summer of 1931. He obtained an offer of a deal from a Hearst magazine which would have brought a total purchase price of $26,000, and although this eventually fell through, the prospect of it would have provided a powerful stimulus toward finishing the book, because the sum was far more than Hammett had ever earned from book publication.[4] Why, then, did he give up the book?

It is true that apart from the title and the names of two characters the story bears little resemblance to the book published in 1934. The setting is San Francisco and the high country north of the city; the narration is again in the third person; and the central character, John Guild, is a private detective frequently referred to as "the dark man." In ten short chapters we learn that Walter Irving Wynant (Clyde in the published book) appears to have shot his secretary and possible mistress, Columbia Forrest, at his home in the mountains and then disappeared. Guild has been employed by an insurance company to find out why and how a check for $10,000, deposited by Wynant and then withdrawn, has been altered from the original $1,000. The trail takes him back to the city and to an interview with Charles Fremont, who says that he was about to marry Columbia and that Wynant was frantically jealous. The idea that Wynant killed her, and intends to kill Fremont also, is strengthened when somebody takes a potshot at Fremont in Guild's presence. In the later chapters it is established that Columbia had a room in the city under the name Laura Porter and that it was Laura Porter in whose favor the checks clearing Wynant's account were drawn. Later Charles Fremont's body is discovered, an apparent suicide. His sister Elsa insists that he cannot have killed Columbia. "He didn't kill her, but he committed suicide," Guild says. "That don't make sense too."[5]

One can only conjecture how the story would have developed, although it is almost certain that, as in the later completed novel, Wynant is in fact dead in spite of apparent successive proofs that he is alive. (This idea may have been derived from Sheridan Le Fanu's nineteenth-century novel, *Wylder's Hand*, in which it is brilliantly exploited.) One is inclined to suspect Elsa Fremont because she is red-haired, often a sign of lethal behavior in Hammett women. It seems likely that Chris, a book reviewer friend of Guild's, is meant to play a vital part in the case. As usual, there are some private jokes. Wynant, well over six feet, weighing no more than 130 pounds and tubercular, resembles his creator. Chris invites Guild to write reviews of detective stories for his paper, under the heading "The Detective Looks at Detective Fiction." Laura Porter's room is at 1157 Leavenworth, and Hammett when his fortunes were on the way up had an apartment at 1155. Although the fragment shows that the book was carefully plotted, the likely reason for its abandonment is that it was disappointing to the writer, as it is for the reader.

Hammett's stylistic objective here would seem to have been an extreme sobriety of tone, both to point up the violence and to make its sensationalism seem more realistic. Guild is shown as a hard man, although not necessarily a shifty one, and the contrast between him and a youthful, fresh-faced district attorney who is deferential toward the knowledgeable detective is nicely managed. Guild has the hard shell common to Hammett detectives, so that Elsa Fremont at one point asks him: "Aren't you sexually human?" and complains that trying to make contact with him is like trying to hold a handful of smoke.[6] At least in these chapters, however, Guild is a much less distinctive figure than Spade, Beaumont, or even the Op. The avoidance of slang and argot, the deliberately commonplace quality of the dialogue, gives a feeling of lifelessness to the writing. The revelations of character through dialogue that marked the two previous books are lacking, and on the evidence we have, the completed book would have been no more than an efficient mystery story. Hammett told Hellman that the book would be, "God willing, my last detective novel,"[7] with the implication that afterward he would write something more serious, but he cannot have wanted it to be inferior to the earlier books. It is likely that he sensed its failure to achieve the greater realism and narrative directness at which he was aiming.

The parties went on; the drinking went on; the money ran out. She and Hammett were, Hellman says, very broke. He turned again to short stories, encouraged by the fact that his agent was able to get as much as $2,500 for one. In 1932 he produced three Sam Spade stories for *American Magazine* and *Collier's*. One of them, "A Man Called Spade,"[8] contains reasonably good, crisp conversation. "They Can Only Hang You Once"[9] gives the information that Spade's age is thirty-eight and has the excellent opening line "Samuel Spade said 'My name is Ronald Ames,'" but these tales cannot have been given much thought or have taken much of their writer's time. In them Spade is just another detective, lacking style or individuality. Much better are "Night Shade" and "Albert Pastor at Home,"[10] two very short stories that contain no detection. The first is a tart, neat tale told in the first person, in which it is revealed at the end that the narrator, who has brought an upper-class white girl into a bar for blacks, is black himself. We have been led to assume that he is white, but when the girl has gone, the barman reminds him that "it don't make no difference how light your skin is or how many colleges you went to, you're still nigger." The response is: "What do you suppose I want to be? A Chinaman?" The second story is about an ex-boxer who breaks up a protection racket on a visit to his hometown. The apparent hero is revealed at the end as a man who runs a similar racket in the big city. These clever stories with their O. Henry twists at the end (but sardonic where O. Henry's endings are often sentimenal) rank among Hammett's best work outside the crime field.

The stories, however, eased the financial pressure only temporarily. Wherever the money went, it was not to Hammett's family, for in 1932 Jose wrote to Knopf complaining that her husband had sent her only one hundred dollars in seven months. The publisher was clamoring for a new book, and Hammett set out to produce one. He moved out of the expensive Hotel Pierre and into the Sutton Club Hotel on East 56th Street, managed by Nathanael West, who was struggling to maintain himself while finishing his second novel, *Miss Lonelyhearts*. The place was cheap; other literary figures, including Edmund Wilson and James T. Farrell, also stayed there, and Hammett took what was jokingly called the Diplomat's Suite, although according to Hellman "even the smallest Oriental could not have functioned well in the space."[11] There he settled down to work. Hellman has given a memorable account of it:

> I had known Dash when he was writing short stories, but I had never been around for a long piece of work. Life changed: the drinking stopped, the parties were over. The locking-in time had come and nothing was allowed to disturb it until the book was finished. I had never seen anybody work that way: the care for every word, the pride in the neatness of the typed page itself, the refusal for ten days or two weeks to go out even for a walk for fear something would be lost. It was a good year for me and I learned from it and was, perhaps, a little frightened by a man who now did not need me.[12]

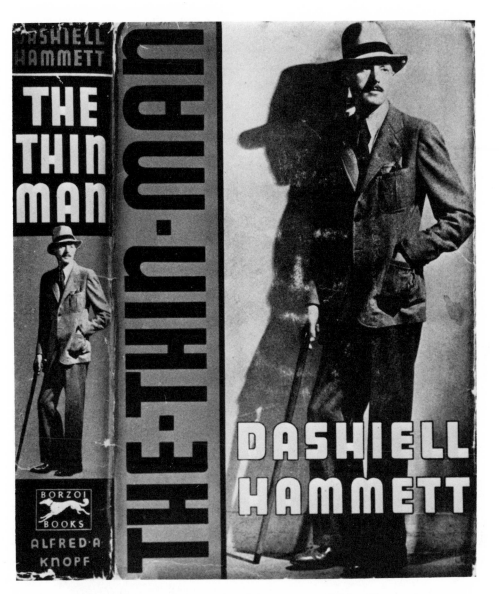

The Thin Man, *published by Knopf, January 1934* (Richard Layman)

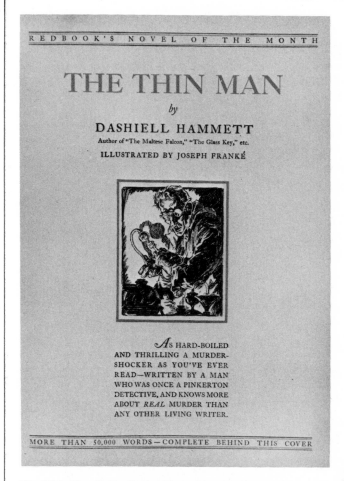

The Thin Man *in* Redbook, *December 1933* (Richard Layman)

The Thin Man was not finished with quite the speed that that quotation suggests, but it was in Knopf's hands by May 1933. When Hammett had complained about the jacket copy for *The Glass Key*, Knopf had suggested that the author write his own the next time. He did so, and he included a photograph of himself wearing a tweed suit and a wide-brimmed hat, carrying a cane, a model of casual elegance. The reviews were good, although less enthusiastic than they had been for some of the earlier books. Sales, however, were the best yet—34,000 copies were sold within eighteen months of publication. Magazine rights proved hard to sell for reasons given below, but *Redbook* eventually bought the story for $5,000. What was to prove in every respect the most vital sale was that of the film rights to MGM for more than $20,000. It was to shape Hammett's future.

The Thin Man differs in style, approach, and feeling from the books before it. The setting is New York, a city of parties rather than people, of drinking rather than discussion. The narrator, Nick Charles (his name is really Charalambides), is an ex-detective who has married Nora, a lumber heiress. Nora is fascinated by detective work and by the eccentric, shady, or downright villainous people encountered in it. (Hellman was always asking Hammett about his detective past and urging him, not quite seriously, to do a little detecting in the present.) Nick, who might be described as a soft and shifty man in contrast to Spade and Beaumont, doesn't care for detection because it is time spent away from drinking. He is first seen leaning against the bar in a 52nd Street speakeasy waiting for Nora to finish her Christmas shopping. They have a dog named Asta, who does whimsical things like knocking over a table of toys at Lord & Taylor and licking a fat woman's leg in Saks. Nick and Nora move from party to party, drinking with people they sometimes hardly know and often don't much like. Wynant has been changed from a philosopher in the first version to an inventor in this one, Guild from a private detective to a policeman who is charmed by Nora. All three deaths in the completed novel take place off-stage, and almost the only violent action occurs when Nick is nicked by a bullet from a gangster named Morelli. Before throwing a pillow at Morelli to disturb his aim Nick knocks Nora across the room to get her out of harm's way, and she is indignant. "You damned fool, you didn't have to knock me cold," she says. "I knew you'd take him, but I wanted to see it."[13]

Pocketbook editions of the five novels, 1943–1945 (Red Harvest, The Dain Curse, The Glass Key, The Thin Man: UCSD; The Maltese Falcon: Richard Layman)

The Thin Man is light-hearted where the best of the other long stories are serious, flippant where they are caustic, sentimental where they are tough. It presents a humorous version of the life then led by Hammett and Hellman, except that there is no mention of problems about money. The book was dedicated to Hellman, and she was delighted to be told that she was Nora, although disconcerted when Hammett added that she was also "the silly girl in the book and the villainess."[14] The departure from the other novels is radical, and *The Thin Man* has often been called the weakest of the five full-length books. Dispraise, however, has gone too far. Undoubtedly the novel was an easy option for Hammett, an evasion of his own view about taking pieces of life and putting them down directly on paper. In Nick's refusal to consider civic or personal corruption seriously (he is stung to some evidence of emotion only by the sadism of the "villainess," Mimi Jorgensen) there is a denial of the subjects dealt with in *Red Harvest* and *The Glass Key*. Yet after several readings, appreciation of Hammett's adroitness in showing the reader a serious and credible plot within the soufflé of party and other conversations is likely to increase. The affection between Nick and Nora is wholly unstrained and convincing, even though its principal fuel seems to be drink. It is, of course, based on the Hammett-Hellman relationship—their conversations, drinking habits, disregard at this time for anything except themselves, even their ages. (Nick is forty-one and Nora twenty-six, and at the time the book was published Hammett was forty, Hellman twenty-seven.) Whether Hellman was quite so innocent of slang as Nora ("What's a lug, Nicky?") may be doubted.

Basically *The Thin Man* should be regarded as a comedy of contemporary American manners, and viewed in this light it is a sparkling piece of work. The party at the Edges' is full of characters touched off in a couple of phrases: the archaeologist host, proud of his collection of battle-axes, who calls himself a ghoul by profession and inclination ("his only joke, if that is what it was"[15]); and his very small, muddy-complexioned wife, Tip, who perches on things and cocks her head always a little to one side. ("Nora had a theory that once when Edge opened an antique grave, Tip ran out of it. . . ."[16]) Tip believes that all literature written more than twenty years ago is bound for the scrap heap because there is no psychiatry in it. Understated tragedies are glimpsed, such as that of Alice Quinn, whose permanently drunk husband chases "everything that's hot and hollow." When she asks Nick what people think of her, his unsatisfactory reply is "You're like everybody else: some people like you, some people don't, and some have no feeling about it one way or the other."[17] Nick's determined refusal to accept any kind of emotional involvement, even with the pathetic Dorothy Wynant, is emphasized throughout. Although the Nick-Nora relationship shows sentimental streaks, the book has hard jokes and phrases. Morelli calls to a somewhat hunchbacked waiter: "Hey, garsong—you with the boy on your back."[18] The parting shot of a big, sullen girl named Miriam when she walks out on a petty crook is "I don't like crooks, and even if I did, I wouldn't like crooks that are stool-pigeons, and if I liked crooks that are stool-pigeons, I still wouldn't like you."[19]

The book ends on a downbeat note that may be considered social comment. It incidentally evades the need for explanations by delivering them humorously in the course of conversation between Nick and Nora and leaves some ends deliberately untied. As he explains to her what happened, she objects, saying: "This is just a theory, isn't it? . . . That seems so loose. . . . Yes, but. . . . Probably." "Probably," Nick says, is a word you have to use a lot in the detective business. When she asks what will happen to the characters now, he replies: "They'll go on being Mimi and Dorothy and Gilbert just as you and I will go on being us and the Quinns will go on being the Quinns. Murder doesn't round out anybody's life except the murdered's and sometimes the murderer's."[20]

Upon that note of disillusionment the book ends. A transatlantic comparison might be made with Evelyn Waugh's novel about Britain's Bright Young People, *Vile Bodies* (1930). Waugh's book is not a murder mystery, but there is a similar attitude of contempt toward activities which are depicted in a superficially neutral manner. *The Thin Man*'s closest relationship, however, is to Carl Van Vechten's *Parties*. Van Vechten was a fashionable novelist of the twenties who aspired to European sophistication in New York settings, and *Parties* (1930) was his final novel. The title is appropriate, for the characters move from party to party, with no thoughts except drink and sex. On the first page David Westlake (a figure based on F. Scott Fitzgerald) says he has killed a man. A couple of pages later his wife Rilda (Zelda) is on the telephone to say that she is killing herself because David has gone off to Paris with a boy. Between drinking everything from sidecars and manhattans to Pernod, the characters look for a corpse "so David can confess and crash the electric chair."[21] There is no corpse, however, for in a Van Vechten novel the characters are only playing at murder, as they play "the toilet-paper race . . . to see which side can unroll the most within a given time." One of them complains that "nobody we know does anything but drink in this crazy town," and all are oppressed by a feeling of doom even though they are having a wonderful time. Simone Fly is "a slim creature in silver sequins from which protruded, at one end, turquoise blue legs and from the other, extremely slender arms and a chalk-white (almost green) face, with a depraved and formless mouth, intelligent eyes, and a rage of cropped hair. Simone Fly resembled a gay death."[22] The people in *The Thin Man*, Nick and Nora excepted, represent the reality of what Van Vechten saw with reverent romanticism. They may resemble death, but they are not gay.

The comparatively small amount paid for serial rights reflected the nervousness of large-circulation magazines about the book's approach to sex. The sadomasochism in Jeff's beatings of Beaumont in *The Glass Key* is not repeated, but Wynant's young son Gilbert is interested in being "hurt, really hurt,"[23] and complains that hurting yourself is not the same thing. He is also interested in cannibalism, and Nick gives him Duke's *Celebrated Criminal Cases of America* to read, pointing out a two-thousand-word story about a prospector who murdered and ate his companions. Gilbert is disappointed, saying that the story is interesting but isn't a pathological case. Several years after Hammett's death, Hellman was asked why he had included this long piece, which is irrelevant to the story. She replied that he wanted to fill up space. No doubt the answer is true enough as far as it goes, but the question remains: Why this particular extract?

Robert Edenbaum has argued that the book is really concerned with "a wide range of social types spiritually sibling to the Alfred G. Packer of the long entry Gilbert Wynant reads. . . . The man-eaters Mimi, Dorothy and Gilbert Wynant, Christian Jorgensen, Herbert Macauley, the Quinns, the Edges, as well as underworld characters like Shep Morelli and Julia Wolf, are little less cannibalistic than Packer."[24] This is ingenious but not convincing. Several of these characters are no more "cannibalistic" than most of the crooks in the short stories. The sensible answer must be that these suggestions of sadistic sexual activities interested Hammett.

There is other evidence of this interest. At one point, when Nick suspects that Mimi is ill-treating her daughter, he says, "You must come over to our place some time and bring your little white whips."[25] Later, at a family conference with Nick and Nora present, Dorothy tells Nick that Mimi will beat her after they have gone, and when Nora says that Dorothy is coming home with them, Mimi attacks the two women so that Nick has to restrain her. Some of this material was cut out in the magazine serialization, along with phrases used by women about going to the can, Nick's observation that Mimi hates men more than any woman can who isn't a lesbian, hints of Gilbert's incestuous feeling for his mother, and phrases like Nora's laughing injunction when she hears that Nick is going to see Mimi: "Keep your legs crossed."[26] A real furor was caused by her question to Nick after he has restrained Mimi: "Tell me the truth, when you were wrestling with Mimi, didn't you have an erection?" "Oh, a little," he says. She laughs, and comments: "If you aren't a disgusting old lecher."[27] The passage was excised in *Redbook*, but Knopf did not flinch from what was then a controversial reference, declaring in an advertisement: "I don't believe the question on page 192 of Dashiell Hammett's *The Thin Man* has had the slightest influence upon the sale of the book. . . . Twenty thousand people don't buy a book within three weeks to read a five word question."[28] The question was omitted from the English edition. Erections did not exist in English fiction at that time.

9

IN THE MONEY

N O W the good life, or the moneyed life, really began, the years in which the money flowed in and out unceasingly. It must have seemed to Hammett in the years that began in 1934 that he had truly discovered the horn of plenty or the philosopher's stone. In that year his income was more than $80,000, and it remained around $100,000 a year until the end of the decade. The money did not come primarily from books, but from films and their derivatives. In the summer of 1934 the film of *The Thin Man* was released, and was an immediate success. William Powell was Nick, Myrna Loy was Nora, and there was general agreement that the casting could not have been better. The director, W. S. Van Dyke, made the picture in eighteen days, emphasizing comedy and deleting all social comment and sexual daring. There are no little white whips; Mimi is a conventional siren, Dorothy any girl in trouble, Gilbert just an oddball. There is drinking; there are parties; but nothing is done to excess, and the Hays office censor insisted that Nick and Nora must have separate beds. Hammett had

William Powell, Hammett, and director. W. S. Van Dyke, during filming of The Thin Man, *1934*

William Powell and Myrna Loy as Nick and Nora Charles with Asta in The Thin Man, *MGM, 1934* (Culver Pictures)

nothing to do with the film, but Albert Hackett and Frances Goodrich, the husband and wife who wrote the script, used a lot of his dialogue. The result was an expert, continuously lively light comedy with a murder mystery thrown in, something that deserved the worldwide success it achieved.

In the two years following, no fewer than five more films were made which were in some way adapted from Hammett's writings. The story of *Mister Dynamite* has already been told. *Satan Met a Lady* was a remake (but bore very little relation to the original) of *The Maltese Falcon*. Warren William and Bette Davis played the parts of detective and siren. *Woman in the Dark* was a thriller adapted from a late (1933) story which had been written with one or both eyes on film production. *The Glass Key* was made into an interesting although not wholly successful film with George Raft and Edwin Arnold as Beaumont and Madvig and Guinn Williams giving a remarkably realistic performance as the sadistic Jeff. Claire Dodd played Janet Henry, and Ray Milland had a small part as her brother. And, finally, there was *After the Thin Man*, the only one of these films with which Hammett was significantly involved. He had originally conceived this film as a sequel to the novel, with Mimi, Gilbert, and the villain Herbert Macauley all appearing and the setting changed from New York to San Francisco. In a facetious interview he said that somebody would have to die in this sequel, but it would certainly not be Powell or Loy. "None but Frankenstein could eliminate either of these fine people." Who then? "Shall it be poor little Asta, the wire-haired fox terrier? God forbid! It shall not be Asta."[1] But Hunt Stromberg, the MGM producer with whom Hammett was working, disliked the idea of a sequel, and the long treatment that finally emerged was a confused and complicated murder story, retrieved only by the presence of Powell and Loy. The Hackett-Goodrich team wrote the script from Hammett's treatment, and the follow-up achieved a success equal to that of the original. The title, of course, was a misnomer, because the actual thin man was the dead Clyde Wynant, but Powell was by now firmly established in filmmakers' affections as the eponymous hero, even though he was far from thin.

In these years the earth brought forth by handfuls. The adventure story comic strip had been created in 1931 with the appearance of *Dick Tracy*, and Hammett was invited to invent a strip with a new character. He was paid $500 a week by Hearst's King Features to produce *Secret Agent X-9*. The artist was a young man named Alex Raymond. Although

Hammett, George Raft, and director, Frank Tuttle,
during filming of The Glass Key, *Paramount, 1935*

X-9 has been said to contain elements of the Hammett novels, including innocent and double-crossing women, a fat villain, and a super-tough detective, this strip seems much like any other, relying on crudely violent action and lacking style, wit, or any other literary quality. The only attraction this wretched activity held for Hammett was the money. He conceived it and wrote the captions for rather more than a year, after which Raymond produced the story line as well as the drawings. Another comic strip writer for King Features, who was told by the syndicate that his work must be inspected by Hammett, remembered that at their sessions in a New York hotel they would drink a lot and talk about fighters, Pinkerton men, anything except comic strips. Hammett said the young man should go out to California "and grab some of that Hollywood dough," adding that the young man could come up with more good ideas in half an hour "than you'll hear in a month of story conferences out there."[2]

The strip had the distinction of making the Federal Bureau of Investigation aware of Hammett's existence for the first, but not the last, time. The director of the FBI explained to the San Francisco Division that Secret Agent X-9 was said to be a former operative of the Department of Justice, and the series had not been cleared. In reply, a special agent recapitulated Hammett's career briefly, assured the director that Hammett had made no claim that this character had been a department operative, mentioned that "an actor by the name of William Powell" had recently appeared in a film worked on by Hammett, and ended by saying that "he has made considerable money from his detective yarns."[3]

Hammett had considerable experience of story conferences, or rather of missing them. He signed an agreement in 1935 under which he was to serve as a general assistant to producer Hunt Stromberg for $1,000 a week when working on a particular scene or scenes, increased to $1,750 a week when he was required to write "complete continuity, including dialogue for any photo-play."[4] He failed to turn up at meetings and to deliver work on time. A secretary assigned to him by the studio visited his home daily but did little or no work. Sometimes she and Hammett did crossword puzzles together, and sometimes he stayed up in his room. On these latter occasions, obvious prostitutes, often black or Oriental, would pass her as they came downstairs on the way out. When he did not appear at all, she packed up and went home at five o'clock. It is hardly surprising that he

Guinn Williams as Jeff and George Raft as Beaumont in The Glass Key, *Paramount, 1935*

Grosset & Dunlap edition (1942) based on the 1942 Paramount remake of The Glass Key *with Brian Donlevy, Veronica Lake, and Alan Ladd (UCSD)*

OPPOSITE: *Charles Rickman as Senator Henry, George Raft as Beaumont, Claire Dodd as Janet Henry, and Edwin Arnold as Paul Madvig in* The Glass Key, *Paramount, 1935*

was taken off the payroll three times. Yet each time he was reinstated, a tribute to his charm, his celebrity, or both.

If one asked how he spent his time in Hollywood (which was broken by trips, sometimes lengthy, to New York), the answer would be drinking, gambling, and making trouble. Hellman called 1934 a year of heavy drinking for them both, adding that she disliked herself when she drank. For Hammett the two following years showed no diminution in his drinking. Hellman was not with him in Hollywood, and in her absence he slept around. He rented the Harold Lloyd mansion, which had "forty-four rooms, vast gardens, a pool, and tennis courts,"[5] as well as the soda fountain in the basement smashed up by Hellman on the brief visit already mentioned. It was, Hammett said, a good place for parties, and whether at parties of his own or other people's, he was invariably drunk and often aggressive. Nathanael West went to one Hammett party hoping that his host might get him a script-writing assignment but found Hammett less than friendly, telling a young woman that she should leave West alone because "he hasn't got a pot to piss in," and later pretending that West had tried to borrow money from him and saying loudly that he had nothing to lend that week.[6] (Remarkably, however, Hammett praised West's Hollywood novel, *The Day of the Locust*, when it appeared in 1939.)

There are more agreeable stories of his behavior at this time. The director Howard Benedict remembered the help Hammett gave to a sick woman depressed after an operation, by visiting her and sending her little presents. Hammett also remembered the birthdays of friends' children and made sure that they got presents. Sometimes he praised other writers. At a party given by Edward G. Robinson, James M. Cain found his hand being wrung by a wild-looking man "with gray, nearly white, hair, with a funny look in his eye. And he said, my God, he admired me extravagantly, and I said, oh, yes, mutual, likewise I'm sure, and I came to find out it was Dashiell Hammett"—whose books, Cain said afterward, he had not read.[7]

But most of the tales are of lechery or of self-destructiveness under the influence of drink. He installed a naked hooker in the bathroom at a party and sent S. J. Perelman up there. In due time a group of guests followed and found the couple having sex. The upshot of this was that Hammett went off for several days in the company of Perelman's wife, Laura. There is a tale of his having a girl who shared men with her mother. He had a fling with another young woman who broke it off "because of all the

Hammett wrote continuity for Secret Agent X-9 *from
January 1934 through April 1935.*

whores around." He was shy and pleasant when sober, Hollywood friends agreed, but a talkative, quarrelsome drunk.[8] One of the drunken occasions landed him in prison. He and Nunnally Johnson, a scriptwriter who later became celebrated as a producer and director, set out for an evening of hard drinking in Miami Beach, where Johnson was living. They found themselves outside a large department store. A lot of rubble lay around, and Hammett picked up chunks of concrete and threw them at the plate glass windows of the store, cheering when the windows broke. He was arrested, and Johnson spent most of the night trying to raise bail. During these years there were several lawsuits against him, mostly for the recovery of comparatively small bills that had been left unpaid. In January 1936 he broke down and spent some time in the hospital with another dose of gonorrhea. Earlier in the month he attended a *Black Mask* writers' dinner, the only occasion on which Raymond Chandler, then known only as a short story writer for the pulps, met Hammett. "Often wonder why he quit writing after *The Thin Man*," Chandler wrote to a correspondent in 1949. "Met him once only, very nice looking tall quiet gray-haired fearful capacity for Scotch, seemed quite unspoiled to me."[9] In spite of the large sums Hammett had earned, he was short of money and asked Knopf for help. The royalty check he received, for less than $500, must have seemed to him hardly enough for a night on the town. Blanche Knopf improved the occasion by asking about his next novel. She was told that it had been delayed by his work in Hollywood.

In 1934 he wrote what was to be his last published fiction, in the form of three stories that appeared in the popular magazine *Collier's*. None is completely successful, but they show how far he had moved away from the gunplay of the *Black Mask* tales. "Two Sharp Knives" is a well-told story on the familiar theme of murder diagnosed as suicide, and "This Little Pig" is a rather heavy-handed satire on the film industry. The best of the three, "His Brother's Keeper," is a boxing story told in the first person by Kid Bolan, a fighter whose brains are in his fists. The theme is that ancient boxing motif about the manager who arranges for his boy to throw a fight and then changes his mind. (A variant of it had been used in *Red Harvest*.) The original aspect of this particular treatment is that the manager is Kid's brother Louey and that Louey is killed after the fight. The Kid dimly realizes that he is the cause of Louey's death, and reflects: "Why, I would have thrown a million fights for Louey, but how could he know he

Hammett at Hotel Lombard, 1935 (UTA)

"This Little Pig," published by Collier's *in March 1934, was the last Hammett story published during his lifetime.* (William F. Nolan)

Collier's *for March 24, 1934*

She showed me. I said, "It's a cute dance." "And you'll let me do it?" she asked. "No," I replied

This Little Pig

A hard-boiled romance of Hollywood, where, it would seem, they don't all love one another

By Dashiell Hammett

MAX RHINEWIEN'S telegram brought me back from Santa Barbara. He glared at me over his bicarbonate of soda and demanded, "And where've you been?"

"Where'd you wire me? I've been trying to finish a play."

"Is there a picture in it?"

"Why not? You bought Soviet Law, didn't you? And that's a bibliography."

"Never mind," he said, "it's a good title anyway. Listen, Bugs, I want you to hop over to Serrita and——"

"Nothing doing. I've still got nine days coming to me and I want to get the

houses instead of just in the neighbs and the sticks. Listen, Bugs, is Sol Feldman a dope?"

"Not that I know of."

"Exactly. Not that anybody knows of. Well, I happened to hear only last night that they're saying up this The might work him in something along the line that he's a drunk piano player that Gracie—say—is taking along to open a dance-hall in this mining town, and she's got some girls with her and—you know—you can work it up."

"Didn't Paramount try something

He had the decency to seem embarrassed. "Well, if you were in my shoes——" He broke off. "Uh—you know Kitty Doran? This is Bugs Parish."

The small dark girl dimpled and held out her hand. "How do you do?"

Fred growled, "Come on, what's the bad news?"

When I told him he hit the top of the tent and spun there. I had expected him to yell his head off, of course, but he put on a really grand performance.

"YOU know how Max is," I said with soothing intent as soon as I could get a word in. "He hears Feldman's

could trust me, with me this dumb?"[10] The current of sentimentality flowing beneath this very well-written story shows how far Hammett was from solving his problems as a writer determined to transcend the murder mystery genre. The debt to Hemingway is obvious, as it never is in his crime fiction.

By a nice irony it was the crime fiction, then as now, that won him praise. André Malraux called him the technical link between Theodore Dreiser and Ernest Hemingway, and when Gertrude Stein came to Hollywood she made a special request that Hammett be invited to a dinner party given for her. There she engaged him in a long and what for him surely must have been a tedious discussion about the different ways in which men wrote about themselves and women in the nineteenth and twentieth centuries. Hammett was warmed by the sun of such praise from intellectuals but was not deceived by it. When he tried to read his early work again with the idea of revising it, he found the task unendurable. "I bet if I worked hard enough on those few pages I could whittle them down to a phrase," he wrote to Hellman.

Perhaps the most creative thing he did during these years was to encourage and guide her progress as a playwright. His criticism of her (and indeed all other) creative work was ruthless. "Even then I knew that the toughness of his criticism, the coldness of his praise, gave him a certain pleasure," she wrote later. "It came from the most carefully guarded honesty I have ever known."[11] He told her that the first play she had written was no good and urged her to try a novel. When she said that she was more comfortable with the stage, he advised her to work from a basis of fact.

Hammett did not go directly to Hollywood when *The Thin Man* appeared but spent the first months of 1934 with Hellman in Florida. There, she says, they drank (his drinking adventure with Nunnally Johnson occurred at this time) and spent some weeks at a fishing camp in the Keys, "fishing every day, reading every night," and finding that "we got along best without people, in the country."[12] Hammett was a fanatical but selective reader, not much interested in people (he thought it a waste of time to read collections of letters) but passionately concerned with factual studies of nature, history, and mathematics. He had the eagerness for knowledge that marks many of the self-educated. Hellman mentions a year of study on the retina and also books about the vision and language of bees, tying

Hammett with his sister, 1934 (UTA)

Hammett at Hotel Lombard, 1935 (UTA)

Black Mask *dinner, January 1936; seated from left: Arthur Barnes, John K. Butler, Tod Ballard, Horace McCoy, Norbert Davis; standing from left: unknown, Raymond Chandler, Herbert Stinson, Dwight Babcock, Eric Taylor, Hammett (UCLA)*

knots, the snapping turtle, the shore life of the Atlantic, and inland birds. He read also classics of fiction, including *Don Quixote* and *Gil Blas* and ranging from such picaresque work to late Henry James. He once said to James Thurber that the plot of *The Maltese Falcon* resembled that of *The Wings of the Dove*.[13] There were, he remarked, a lot of books he had missed in the San Francisco Public Library.

During this time in Florida, Hellman worked on what became *The Children's Hour*, showing each draft to Hammett as she wrote it. Among the criticisms he made was one which involved the elimination of Judge Potter, an important figure in the early versions. He also suggested a scene in which irate mothers come to take their children away from the school when the scandal breaks. "She wrote it in three months of travail," a newspaper interview recorded. "Hammett read it. Said the whole idea was a mistake and he apologized for offering it."[14] When the play was produced with enormous success in November 1934, Hellman said he felt that all his trouble with her had paid off.

She also wrote her second play, the unsuccessful *Days to Come*, in Hammett's company. They had rented the house of a rich professor at Princeton, and the place was filled every night with "students who liked Hammett, but liked even better the free alcohol and the odd corners where they could sleep and bring their friends." They were, she says, a dull lot, but then "Dash never much examined the people to whom he was talking if he was drunk enough to talk at all."[15] The students and the show business people who also came to drink and sleep alienated the Princeton neighbors, but neither Hammett nor Hellman cared much about what the neighbors thought. About *Days to Come* he was encouraging. The subject bears a distant resemblance to that of *Red Harvest*, with thugs brought in to break a strike in a small Ohio town, but the treatment is altogether different, concentrating on the moral problems involved for the family of the rich, liberal mill owner. The play ends with the defeat of the strike and the return of the workers and was Hellman's first, and very clumsy, attempt to write a play with a social message. The writing, of course, was hers, but Hammett may have been partly responsible for the approach. On stage the play was a disaster, and she was so upset on the first night that she vomited in the theater. The piece closed after seven performances. Hammett said that he had been mistaken about its being a good play but was otherwise consolatory. Soon afterward they left Princeton and went to Hollywood.

Hellman, now a celebrity in her own right, was under contract to work on films for Samuel Goldwyn. Hammett had agreed to come back and write an original story for a third *Thin Man* picture. He had also sold all except radio rights in the *Thin Man* characters to MGM for $40,000.

During the stay at Princeton, Hammett gave an interview to the campus newspaper in which he said that the book he was working on would not be a mystery, adding, "I don't really like detective stories, anyway." The new book would be "about a family of a dozen children out on an island, all of them getting in each other's way. You see, all I do in a story is just get some characters together and then let them get in each other's way."[16] Nothing of this book was written, and the gap between the concept of a serious novel and what Hammett actually did was growing. *The Maltese Falcon* and *The Glass Key* were one thing, the writing of another original story for the *Thin Man* characters quite another.

10

DISCOVERING A CAUSE

I N 1937 Jose Hammett obtained a Mexican divorce by mail, so that neither she nor Hammett had to appear in court. This meant also that the divorce was not recognized in the United States, where she remained his legal wife. Hammett was unaffected emotionally by the divorce, and at this time showed little interest in his wife or his daughters, who remained in Jose's custody. Later he bought her a small stucco house in a middle-class section of Los Angeles, where she lived until her death with her older daughter, Mary.

Hammett, as he told the writers Albert Hackett and Frances Goodrich, had decided to live flamboyantly. He continued to drink a lot and frequently passed out at some point in an evening's drinking. He also continued to gamble (like most gamblers, without making money), gave parties in his hotel suite at the Beverly Wilshire, bedded women, and made loans that he knew would never be repaid. He paid twenty dollars to his barber for a haircut, thirty dollars for a shave. MGM, infuriated by his failure to turn up for script conferences or to deliver work on time, forced him to accept a contract for the new *Thin Man* story under which he would receive payment on results instead of a weekly salary. He got $5,000 for a synopsis, another $10,000 on acceptance of the idea, and a further $20,000 for the complete story.

Another Thin Man (1939), the third film in the series, has a complex plot carried out with great skill. It is lifted from the ruck of ordinary comedy mysteries through a performance of remarkable conviction from Sheldon Leonard as the sinister Phil Church, who appears to be able to cause deaths by dreaming in advance about the victims. Powell and Loy play the charade of marriage and detection with their customary charm, but it is made surprisingly more plausible by the seriousness of Leonard's performance. None of the five later *Thin Man* films matched the first, probably because the original was made from a book written with verve and humor, whereas the sequels were work-for-hire. But *Another Thin Man* is certainly the best of the five. Hammett had nothing to do with the last three of them.

Work on the film did not make him feel cheerful. He argued with Hunt Stromberg and continued to avoid meetings, both with the producer and with the long-suffering Hackett and Goodrich, who were writing the screenplay. But he went on with the work. After all, how else could he have been paid so much money for writing a story of not much more than a hundred pages?

That Hammett viewed what he did with total cynicism was suggested memorably by Nunnally Johnson in a letter written shortly after Hammett's death:

> He saw no more reason to write when he not only had all the money he needed but was assured of all that he would ever need for the remainder of his life. This turned out to be a mistake, but it was a sound enough belief at the time. . . .
>
> Apparently there was nothing in writing that interested him but the money. He had none of the usual incentives that keep writers at their typewriters for as long as they have the strength to hit the keys. He had no impulse to tell any more stories, no ambition to accomplish more as a writer, no interest in keeping his name alive, as it is often de-

scribed, or any other vanity about himself or his work. This is not to say that he was not gratified by the respect with which his stories were received, nor should it be taken to mean that he did not apply to his work all the conscientiousness of a self-respecting craftsman. But once he had made his pile, that was all there was to it. Out went the typewriter and he never wrote another book or story. If there is a precedent for a decision like this in a writer I have never heard of it. . . .

To say that the decision turned out to be a mistake calls for a second explanation, and my testimony on this point I must confess is speculation. . . . From the day I met Hammett, in the late twenties, his behavior could be accounted for only by an assumption that he had no expectation of being alive much beyond Thursday. . . . Once this assumption was accepted, Hammett's way of life made a form of sense. Even allowing for the exuberance of youthfulness and the headiness of the certain approach of success, not to mention the daffiness of the twenties, no one could have spent himself and his money with such recklessness who expected to be alive much longer. For once in my life I knew a man who was clearly convinced that there would never be a tomorrow. . . .

I suppose that by the time he came to realize that he would in all likelihood be here not only next Thursday but for many Thursdays to come it was too late to sit down at the typewriter again with much confidence. When the end approached, it was thirty years later than he had expected it, and Death owed him a genuine apology when eventually it made its tardy appearance.[1]

Johnson's letter states eloquently a case which has often been made. Nobody has suggested better the self-destructive foolishness of Hammett's life once he began to be paid what were for the period immense amounts of money. (His yearly earnings far exceeded those of Fitzgerald at the height of his popularity or later those of Chandler at the zenith of his fame.) It is quite possible that his extraordinary determination to spend more money than he received was partly based upon the belief that he had no more than a year or two to live. But even though Hammett may have said to Johnson that nothing in writing interested him but the money, this was far from the truth.

The whole course of his career from the time that *Red Harvest* was accepted by Knopf tells a different story, that of a man intent upon producing novels equal to the finest work of his contemporaries, an author frustrated not by lack of talent but by a failure of will. He wanted the good life, the rich life, and once it had been given to him by Hollywood, he could not let it go. Yet at the same time he despised the medium in which he worked for the way it softened and trivialized every serious conception, and he disliked particularly his own role in this process. It would be wrong to attribute his drinking to this cause alone, but undoubtedly self-contempt had a share in it. This bitter distaste for the life he led was expressed in a letter to Hellman about the *Thin Man* characters in which he was implicitly critical of their own rackety lives. "Nick loved Nora and Nora loved Nick and everything was just one great big laugh in the midst of other people's trials and tribulations. Maybe there are better writers in the world, but nobody ever invented a more insufferably smug pair of characters."[2] At the end of Van Vechten's *Parties* Rilda says to David, "There are actually people who believe that because a person is well-fed he has no problems," and David replies, "We're here because we're here, and we should be extremely silly not to make the worst of it."[3] Hammett detested this attitude, yet it was not far from his own. That "On the Make" should have been turned into *Mister Dynamite* was bad enough, but that his way of life should depend on the success of Nick and Nora was intolerable. Yet he took the money.

He also thought and talked about writing his novel. Knopf had tired of the erratic author and relieved him from his contract, but Bennett Cerf at Random House was prepared to make what he must have known was the speculation of a $5,000 advance. Alfred Knopf said that Hammett was a terrible man and that Cerf would have nothing but trouble with him. The book he was writing, or perhaps not writing, was called *My Brother Felix*, and later it was even announced for publication as *There Was a Young Man*. But although Hammett told a friend that he had written more than 160 pages, this may have been overstatement. No more than a few pages remain at the Hammett archive in the Humanities Research Center of the University of Texas in Austin. Apart from the failure to produce a book, however, Cerf had no particular trouble with his author. In fact, Hammett returned the advance when after two years he had not produced a novel, saying that he was afraid he would never write it.

The exact time at which Hammett became active in politics remains uncertain. The author of *Red Harvest* and *The Glass Key* was certainly aware of political and civic corruption, but the conclusion might be drawn from those books that these were inevitable components of American life. Perhaps his misplaced enthusiasm for *Days to Come* was rooted in a feeling for the American labor movement. The first real evidence of his active concern with politics, however, came with the Spanish Civil War.

The war broke out in July 1936 with the revolt of right-wing parties headed by General Franco against the newly elected government, which was left-wing but far from Communist. The Franco revolt received very material help, including bombers and later troops, from Hitler's Germany and Mussolini's Italy. The government was supported more cautiously by Stalin's Soviet Union, with material help in the form of tanks, planes, and a small number of troops, accompanied by commissars who played an important part in reshaping the government and army. Stalin was interested in a Communist-controlled Spain, not in a republican victory. As a precautionary measure some seventy percent of Spanish gold reserves were sent to the Soviet Union for safekeeping, a keeping so safe that they were never seen again. Russian policy throughout the war, which ended in early 1939 with total republican defeat and the ascendancy of Franco and the fascist *Falange Española*, was to eliminate all groups hostile to communism. The semi-Marxist, semi-Trotskyite *Partido Obrero de Unificación Marxista* (POUM) was destroyed, and its leaders killed, and many thought the Communist party responsible for the death of the anarchist leader Durruti. The Spanish Communists were a small group when the war began. Before it ended, they held almost total sway over a feeble government, and their inefficient generals and Russian advisers controlled most of the army. The effect of Stalin's intervention in Spain, with its ruthless destruction of parties and individuals opposed to Communist party rule, was a deadly one.

All this is known now, but what liberals and socialists in other countries saw at the time was a legally elected government struggling to put down a fascist-supported rebellion, with the Soviet Union apparently on the side of the angels. The cause of republican Spain fired a spirit of idealism in the youth of other countries, in support not of a nation but of a cause felt to be quite certainly good. Volunteers ready to fight and die for the republic and against fascism came in thousands from all over Europe. In Britain they included George Orwell, who was wounded, and the poet and Marxist theoretician Christopher Caudwell, who was killed. The American volunteers formed the Abraham Lincoln Brigade, and they had the financial support—although rarely the personal participation—of many writers and artists. The emotional impact of the war went far beyond the fate of the three thousand-odd American volunteers, many of whom were killed or wounded. To many it seemed that the best hopes of European socialism died, for a generation or more, in Spain.

Liberals in the Hollywood community participated enthusiastically in raising funds for the republic. Hammett contributed to a medical fund for wounded Americans and also put up some money for the making of Joris Ivens' documentary *Spanish Earth*, in which Hemingway collaborated. When the film was privately screened at the house of the film actor Fredric March, Hammett and Hellman attended along with Fitzgerald and Hemingway, who introduced the film. Later they went on to drinks with Dorothy Parker, and Hammett insisted drunkenly (but perhaps correctly) that Hemingway put women into his books only so that they could admire him.[4] The relationship between the two men was never easy. When Hellman told Hammett that Hemingway liked his books, he laughed and said it must mean that he was a bad writer.[5] She records another occasion, just after the Spanish Civil War had ended, when the two men, both fairly drunk, became involved in an argument in New York's Stork Club about the importance of saving intellectuals from Franco's prisons. Hemingway jeered at people safe in New York; Hammett expressed his dislike for being lectured; Hemingway bent a spoon between his bicep and forearm and challenged Hammett to do so; Hammett told him to go back to bullying Fitzgerald, added that when he had done things like spoon bending it was for Pinkerton money, and ended: "Why don't you go roll a hoop in the park?"[6] One may suspect Hellman of improving the scene a little, but not of inventing it. There is a rumor that Hammett wanted to visit Spain but that the American Communist party thought it inadvisable. If it were true, that would mean he was a party member, something that has never been positively confirmed.

Hammett's interest in politics was not confined to Spain. He signed, along with many other writers, including Hellman, a statement justifying the Moscow trials of old Bolshevik leaders and applauding the trials as measures that would free the Soviet Union from "insidious internal dangers, principal menace to peace and democracy."[7] It is true that the signatories did not then know of, or refused to believe, the murder and starvation of millions in the Soviet Union. But the evidence was so often contradictory and the crimes of which Bukharin, Zinoviev, Kamenev, Radek, and, of course, the absent Trotsky were accused were so ridiculous that they could be accepted only as a gesture of belief, not as an act of reason. Such a gesture of belief Hammett was prepared to make. Others made it, too, but most lacked his skeptical intelligence. He came to an acceptance of communism by reading Hegel and Marx, rather than from an instinctive belief that all men are brothers, an idea which his experience of life contradicted. It is as though he was taking his revenge for writing about Nick and Nora by staying faithful, as he was to do for years, to an autocracy that would immediately have committed his two characters, and most of their friends, to labor camps. If he contemplated the idea that in the Soviet Union he also would probably have ended up in a camp, he accepted that, too. His awareness of the horrors of German Nazism may have spurred him on to speak at Communist-sponsored anti-Nazi rallies. Certainly, although he consistently supported the Soviet Union, he had few illusions about it. When Hellman was invited to a Moscow theater festival in 1937 and suggested that he might like to accompany her, he refused. She would have, he told her, a good wasted time.[8]

A lot of his energies now were occupied by political activity, and there is no doubt about his interest in what he was doing. Yet it is likely that this activity served also as an excuse for not working on a novel. The many amusing, sometimes witty letters he wrote to Hellman at the time concern gossip about friends and acquaintances, what journalists were saying about this and that, and who was insulting whom. About the photos *Life* published of Hellman, a bad one playing tennis, a good one knitting, he quipped, "So I guess you're more the domestic type."[9] Only casually does he mention that "the Guild has been signing up an average of about twelve members a week."

The guild was the Screen Writers Guild, of which he was a prominent member. It had been formed to give members power to negotiate their contracts through a union, rather than by means of the studio-backed Screen Playwrights. The battle was long and bitter, with his employer, MGM, one of the principal opponents. He suggested to the apolitical

Hammett addressing anti-Nazi rally, mid-1930s (UTA)

Hammett with Dorothy Parker at anti-Nazi rally, mid-1930s (UTA)

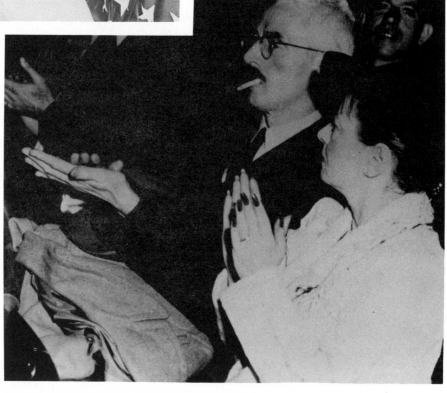

Fitzgerald, who is likely to have flinched from the prospect, that he join "a studio committee for democratic action," which would work to unseat the Republican governor of California, Frank Finley Merriam, in November 1938. (A similar letter was probably sent to other writers.) This pursuit of political ends must have been a further irritant to MGM when it considered his irresponsibility in relation to studio work; his days of earning $80,000 a year in Hollywood came to an end in 1938, and his MGM contract ended finally in July 1939. After that he was offered various writing assignments. The only one he accepted, in 1950, was never fulfilled.

He probably felt relief at the termination of a contract he would never have ended himself. In the latter part of 1938 he came east and worked with Hellman on *The Little Foxes*, while recuperating from an illness that was probably alcoholic in origin. This brilliant piece about enmities in a southern family, arguably Hellman's most successful play, had its origins in her own early life in New Orleans. It was, for that reason, peculiarly difficult for her to write, with reality constantly getting in the way of fiction. "In the first three versions of the play, because it had been true in life, Horace Giddens had syphilis,"[10] she later wrote, and it took her a long time to see that this was artistically damaging. Hammett coaxed and bullied her through those three drafts, and several more. When she threatened to abandon the play, he said calmly that nobody but the two of them would care if it were finished or not. She was on the eighth version when he "gave a nod of approval," although suggesting that she should cut out the "blackamoor chitchat."[11] With the blackamoor chitchat duly removed the play was produced in early 1939, with Tallulah Bankhead in the part of Regina that Bette Davis would play on the screen. It was an instant and immense success.

It would be wrong to say that Hammett and Hellman collaborated on a play or screenplay, but she almost always asked for, and often took, his advice. Their nearest approach to collaboration came in 1941 when Warner Brothers bought the rights to Hellman's successful play *Watch on the Rhine*. Hammett wrote the screenplay, and Hellman by her own account then "edited" it. The screen credit said that she supplied "additional scenes and dialogue," and it is clear that they worked closely together.[12]

From 1940 onward, political activities became increasingly important to Hammett, although the outbreak of European war in September 1939

Lillian Hellman, mid-to-late-1930s (Ben Pinchot Photo, New York Public Library)

Lillian Hellman, Talullah Bankhead, and producer, Herman Schumlin, during rehearsal of The Little Foxes, *ca. 1939* (Vandamm Photo, New York Public Library)

did not at first greatly concern him. As national chairman of a Communist-front organization called the Committee on Election Rights, he tried to act as spearhead for national protests against minority parties being excluded from the ballot "through terror, intimidation and arrest of ordinary citizens."[13] It was no doubt natural that he should come again to the attention of the FBI. "Dashiell Hammett is wearing himself thin trying to prevent the Communist party being ruled off the ballot in New York," one memorandum said, quoting an "unknown source." It added that although passing himself off as independent he had "deluged" New York unions with telegrams urging support of Earl Browder, the Communist candidate in the presidential election. His pronouncements in speeches, letters, and articles faithfully followed the party line, which was isolationist. With Hitler's invasion of the Soviet Union in June 1941, this position changed abruptly to a demand for American involvement in the war and, when such involvement had been compelled by the Japanese attack on Pearl Harbor, for the opening of a second front in Western Europe to relieve pressure on Russia. Thus, in early 1940 Hammett condemned the "war hysteria" of the Roosevelt administration. He was still opposing the "criminal" and "imperialist" war in June 1941. By September, however, he was sponsoring the Americans All Week, designed to "promote national unity for the defeat of Hitlerism" by eliminating discrimination against foreign-born Americans, and in December the League of American Writers, of which he was president, announced that it "proudly supports the President and Congress in the Declaration of War on Fascist Japan," and urged the declaration of war against Germany and Italy which followed.[14]

There is nothing unusual in such Communist about-turns, but it is shameful that a man of Hammett's independent mind should have behaved like any party hack. Such behavior even extended to the characteristic denial of free speech to other opposition groups. When an objector at one meeting held in 1940 protested against the party's denial of election and civil rights to the Socialist party, he was hissed, and Hammett, in his role as chairman, said that only anti-democratic elements benefited from disturbing unity in such a way.[15] Then and thereafter, the abnegation of his will in relation to the current party line was total.

It is ironic that in 1941, at a time when Hammett's connection with Hollywood had ended, much the best film version of any Hammett book

DASHIELL HAMMETT

July 24, 1941

Dear Friend:

The funds you have contributed to the Exiled Writers Committee of the League of American Writers for the rescue of anti-Nazi refugee writers are at last bearing fruit.

But ----

A few weeks ago, Anna Seghers and her family landed in Vera Cruz without money enough to complete their flight, although the Exiled Writers Committee emptied its pockets to cover the last mile.

Last week eight other anti-Nazi writers reached Ellis Island, only to be held there by a ruling which prevents aliens of Axis nationality from entering or leaving or passing through the country. If they are not to be detained there indefinitely, or even sent back to overseas camps, we must meet the legal expenses of presenting their cases in Washington.

If all the long work in which you have helped us is not to prove futile, the Exiled Writers Committee must complete the cases it has undertaken. Others are on the way; others yet are still in concentration camps. For these we must

--- continue to send food.

--- be ready to buy passage whenever a way out opens, and the situation changes daily.

--- be able at all times to meet emergencies as they arise.

The Committee must raise $5,000. within the next few weeks. Will you mail me TODAY your contribution toward the final solution of these problems -- legal fees, food, clothing, medicine, transportation, - Life? Will you add the last miles to the thousands that these anti-fascist writers have already travelled?

Please make your check payable to Dashiell Hammett, and mail in the enclosed envelope.

Very sincerely yours,

Dashiell Hammett

DASHIELL HAMMETT

room 1115
381 Fourth Avenue
New York City

*Plea sent by Hammett
as President of the
League of American
Writers, 1941*

was made. The director and moving spirit in this third version of *The Maltese Falcon* was John Huston, who had recently come to Warner Brothers. He sensibly adapted the film himself, keeping a great deal of the book's dialogue, and, when George Raft declined the chance to play Sam Spade (perhaps he remembered the cool reception given to *The Glass Key* a few years earlier), chose Humphrey Bogart, who gave perhaps the best performance of his career. Another inspired choice was Sidney Greenstreet as Gutman. Greenstreet was a stage actor who had never appeared in the movies, but after this film was much in demand for parts that required a chuckling, apparently amiable villain. Some of the other casting was similarly brilliant, in particular Peter Lorre as Cairo and Elisha Cook, Jr., as Wilmer. Only Mary Astor was miscast, giving the ice of Brigid but never the fire beneath. Nevertheless, the film remains a classic thriller after more than forty years.

A classic thriller—but the very phrase suggests how far the film was from realizing the book's potential. In fairness to Huston it should be said that the Hollywood of the early forties found much of Hammett unacceptable. Just as the nearly pathological Wynants of *The Thin Man* had to be turned into mere eccentrics, so the ambiguities and gamey sexual quality of *The Maltese Falcon* disappeared. Wilmer is no longer Gutman's boy, Cairo is a primping popinjay but not an obvious homosexual, and the ambience of guarded mistrust between Spade and the police has become conventional opposition. Most diluted of all is the character of Spade himself. Bogart's excellence in the part does not extend, was not permitted by Hollywood ethics to extend, to the subtleties suggested in the book. We never doubt that this Sam Spade is honest, however toughly he may talk.

The film's success can have been of only minor interest to Hammett. He was eager to play a part in the war, and in early October 1942 an alarm was sounded by J. Edgar Hoover in an FBI memorandum sent by special messenger to the chief of the Military Intelligence Service in the War Department: Dashiell Hammett, "reported to this Bureau as being a Communist Party sympathizer," had enlisted in the army the previous month.[16] The official reply was that the files did not show him as a member of the military establishment or a civilian employee and that, therefore, no action was contemplated. The FBI then, to its dismay, lost track of Hammett for two years. Not until April 1944 did it finally confirm

Lobby sheet for the third film treatment of The Maltese Falcon, *Warner Bros., 1941*

Mary Astor as Brigid and Humphrey Bogart as Spade in The Maltese Falcon, *Warner Bros., 1941*

Bogart as Spade, Sidney Greenstreet as Gutman, Peter Lorre as Cairo, and Mary Astor as Brigid in The Maltese Falcon, *Warner Bros., 1941*

Movie poster for The Maltese Falcon, *Warner Bros., 1941*

that Samuel Dashiell Hammett had enlisted as a private in September 1942, weighing 141 pounds, standing 6 feet 1¾ inches tall, and having a divorced wife, Josephine. Even this report was incorrect, for it gave Hammett not two daughters but one daughter and a son named Joseph. He was now to be found, a further report said, in Anchorage, Alaska, and "at the present time a casual surveillance is being maintained."[17]

11

THE ARMY
AND AFTER

GIVEN Hammett's adherence to the Communist party line, it made sense that he should support the war as soon as the United States was (to put it in his terms) fighting on the side of the Soviet Union. He was also moved, however, by a desire for involvement in physical action and a liking for the company of men. He may also have felt that the regimentation of army life and enforced activity would rid him of the need to think about his unwritten novel.

It is astonishing that, at the age of forty-eight and with his health record, he was ever accepted for army service. In fact, he was rejected three times and was finally accepted only after he agreed to have some of his badly decayed teeth taken out. After some months in Fort Monmouth, New Jersey, no more than twenty miles from New York, and a few weeks elsewhere, he was finally assigned to the barren volcanic island of Adak, eight hundred miles from the Alaskan mainland. He spent the rest of the war there and was discharged in September 1945 as a master sergeant, with the Asiatic-Pacific Medal, four Overseas Bars, and a Good Conduct Medal.

Hammett reporting for duty, 1942 (*New York* Daily News)

According to Richard Layman, there was "an unusual concentration of suspected subversives" on Adak, and he considers it likely that Hammett was sent there because of his political background. Against this view is the fact that he was allowed to found and edit a camp newspaper, called the *Adakian*. The paper's purpose, an editorial in the first issue said, was "to give the Adak soldier—every morning—a paper that he will like to read and that will keep him as up-to-date as possible on what's going on in his world."[1] The aim was fulfilled, with some help from Hammett's subscriptions to news magazines and the *New York Times*. No attempt was made to express a political viewpoint, either in editorials or in his few signed articles.

Hammett was also given the assignment, with another soldier who had fought as a member of the Lincoln Brigade in the Spanish Civil War, of producing an official booklet, eventually published as *The Battle of the Aleutians*, about the progress of the war as it affected the Aleutian chain. The coauthor produced a draft written from a left-wing viewpoint, which Hammett rewrote, draining off the political flavor so that the final result was almost wholly factual. Further—and this seems another indication that whether or not he was sent to the Aleutians as a suspected subversive, he was trusted by the army authorities there—he was sent on a morale-boosting lecture tour to the various army camps. He estimated that he had done almost ten thousand miles of flying around the islands. On the Alaskan mainland, he spent some time at Anchorage, the nearest approach to ordinary American civilization in Alaska. There he went on a tremendous drinking spree, in the course of which he bought one of the bars. At the end of the war he gave it to the black woman who ran it for him.

Hellman said Hammett told her that the happiest day of his life was the day of his acceptance by the army.[2] Whether or not he used those words, he clearly enjoyed army life. He liked the hard conditions, telling her in one of many affectionate letters: "I am big strong man who throw out the chest and laugh at war 'ha ha'! and stride over tundra baring upper plate to wind and rain."[3] In another letter he said he looked like God's older brother. He wrote comically about the problem of urinating in the latrines because of the powerful winds; as another soldier observed, if you did not crawl rather than walk to the latrines, the wind would take you to Siberia. He said that most of the soldiers kept their eyes down, because of the slippery footing and no doubt to avoid the wind. By contrast, he positively enjoyed walking across the tundra against the wind and once exhorted a companion to raise his eyes and look at Mount Moffit, "clean and lovely against the sky."[4] After the war he suggested to Hellman, with apparent seriousness, that they live in the Aleutians.

Hammett also wrote Hellman about a play on which she was working: "I think we're going to have to make a rule that you're not to tackle any work when I'm not around to spur, quiet, goad, pacify and tease you. . . . It is obvious that you're not capable of handling yourself."[5] And while in the Aleutians he rediscovered his family, in particular his younger daughter, Jo. In 1941, when the sisters paid him a visit in New York, he was infuriated by Mary's account of her wild life in California and gave her a black eye. To Jo, however, he was tender, writing on her birthday in 1944: "So now you're eighteen and I'm all out of child daughters. My family is cluttered with grown women. There's nobody who has to say 'Sir' to me anymore and there are no more noses to wipe."[6] It is true, however, that he had not wiped any childish noses for years.

These letter-writing activities still left him with some leisure time. He read Auden, Simenon, and Heine among others and reread Marx. And he enjoyed, perhaps more than anything else, the evident affection of many young soldiers for God's older brother, whom they called Pop. They liked his choice of two blacks among the eight people who worked on *The Adakian*. They admired the independent attitude toward officers exemplified by his reply to one who had come to inspect the paper: "If you have a complaint, major, take it to the general."[7] And they envied the wealth that made it unnecessary for him to cash army paychecks. He lent them money, gave them advice when asked, listened to their complaints about needing a woman, and said eventually: "If you kiddies don't stop this stuff I'm going to move."[8] His fiftieth birthday was celebrated in *The Adakian* by the headline "Hammett Hits Half-Century," followed by "Half-Century Claims Foul."[9]

He wrote nothing outside his army work and letters but told Hellman and others that he was thinking about a novel. It would concern a man who came home from the war and did not like his family, and the title would be "The Valley Sheep Are Fatter." The book, however, got no further than a number of index cards about characters and plot. There would be plenty of time, he perhaps reflected, when the war was over.

But when it ended and he received his discharge, he did not write the

Hammett with the staff of The Adakian
(William Glackin)

Hammett in the Aleutians, 1944 (Robert
Colodny)

DH

FROM DH's PROSPECTUS—

I am against people who push other people around and it's quieter with a knife. I am against Freud and Deceit and Abbott and Costello and the Articles of War and $50,000 offers. I am for people who are kind and courageous and honest and willing to bet on the second front. I do not believe that all mankind's problems are being solved but what do you expect in 50 years? I am in dead earnest about this. Dead. I am an American and I prefer democracy to any other form of government including Hammettism. Shut up.

VOL I Number 50   SATURDAY 27 MAY 1944

HAMMET HITS HALF CENTURY

50 YEARS AGO TODAY

By R. Harvey Jack

At the same time that the wireless was born in Italy a little bundle of joy? was born in St. Mary's County, Md. named Dashiell Hammett. Many renowned personages call it pre-destination that these 2 "live wires" should occur at the same time. Since then "Sam" has attained great heights in the field of writing his greatest, perhaps, being editor of the local island newspaper.

MOUNTBATTEN RESIGNS

Kandy, Ceylon, May 27 (AP) --Admiral Lord Louis Mountbatten resigned today "as a protest against the unsportsmanlike criticism" of Dashiell Hammett, Aleutian editor.

When asked for comment, Hammett laughed heartily.

LGREEN'S DRUG

DASHIELL HAMMETT'S AUTOGRAPH

FREE WITH EACH SUNDAE

—OLIVER PEDIGO

NEW WALGREEN'S FOR HAMMETT

Pittsburgh, May 27 (AP)-- Pittsburgh marked the 50th birthday of Dashiell Hammett, protege of R. Harvey Jack, local composer, musician, bookkeeper, typist and gambler, by opening a new Walgreen's today in his honor.

Whose honor?

Jack wired from the Aleutians that he had broken a champagne bottle over Hammett's head.

HALF-CENTURY CLAIMS FOUL

Somewhere in the Aleutians, May 27 (AP)--T/5 Dashiell Hammett is 50 today.

The author of "Blood Money" and former war correspondent for Godey's Lady's Book observed the occasion with a quiet scream and a light repast with his Aleutian haunt.

A few Friends (few people know that Hammett is a Quaker) joined him in a simple birthday feast of AP dispatches garnished with the heads of old mimeograph operators. Correction fluid and blood were served.

Congratulatory wires poured in from all corners of Four Corners, Idaho.

The regular Russian communique reported no important changes on the land front.

> CRACK

CPL BERNARD ANASTASIA '44

May 27, 1944, edition of **The Adakian,** *celebrating Hammett's fiftieth birthday*

novel. There was no financial need to do so, for no fewer than three weekly serials derived from his work were on the radio. One was based on *The Thin Man* and another on *The Maltese Falcon.* The third involved a new heavyweight detective called (rather confusingly, because Caspar Gutman had been similarly named) *The Fat Man.* Hammett may have conceived the character of this new fat man, Brad Runyon, but otherwise he had nothing to do with the series, which brought in $1,300 a week. His income was little less than it had been when he worked in Hollywood.

Meanwhile, Hellman had bought a house on fashionable East 82nd Street in New York and an estate in Westchester County named Hardscrabble Farm, which had 130 acres of ground. Hammett had his own small apartment on East 66th Street and after his discharge divided his time between New York and the farm. For a short while he seems to have made an attempt to change the way he lived, to cut down on his drinking and to avoid involvement in politics. The FBI noted that "during his service in the Army there was no evidence of Communist activity."[10] And now he told Hellman, who must have been disconcerted (for although she never carried a party card she was a faithful believer in the virtues of Stalin's Soviet Union), that she should suspend judgment on the abilities of Harry Truman as president. Later he was scathing about her political support for the man he called the Iowa yogi, Henry Wallace. But within months, perhaps within weeks, he was drinking hard again, hard and with a kind of desperation.

No doubt the despair sprang from his inability to write. He might write to Jo that "it's swell having a new novel not to do. I was getting pretty bored with just not working on that half a dozen or so old ones,"[11] but these were the words of a man who saw so little ahead of him that on most days, as he said, he felt no need to get up in the morning. He clung to Mary and Jo in a strange, violent, sometimes almost hostile way. When Jo got married, he went to Los Angeles for the wedding, got drunk, and wept because he had no sons. All this and more was forgiven him, by Jo in particular, and by friends. In a Chicago restaurant he once ordered everything on the menu. More and more often he was drunk, sleeping through parties or out in the street. "Drunk, in the gutter, and it was disgusting. He was a disgusting drunk," one friend said.[12]

At other times he remembered that he was a country boy. He loved Hardscrabble Farm and the life that could be led there. He read widely

Hammett with Hellman at "21," 1945 (George Karger, *Life* Magazine © 1973 Time, Inc.)

and seriously, fished, sailed and hunted, put up bird houses and feeding boxes. But he disliked the steady stream of visitors who came to the farm, most of them theater people and crackpot, or at least impractical, politicians, and he found it was no longer a place where he could stay with pleasure. He parted from Hellman, perhaps because he turned up dead drunk at the opening night of her play *Another Part of the Forest*, perhaps because of his open admiration for Patricia Neal, who played the young Regina Hubbard. He took an apartment in Greenwich Village, hired a black housekeeper named Rose Evans, who looked after him as if he were an errant son, and had a woman sleeping in the apartment on most nights. He went on drinking. He did no work.

The FBI had not abandoned interest in him, although in 1945 his name was deleted as a "Key Figure" in relation to Communist activities. A watch was kept on Hardscrabble Farm, even though the size of the grounds made it "difficult to conduct investigation in that area."[13] The local police department was approached and advised the FBI that they had no record concerning Hammett. An informant said that he had not been active in village meetings. A watchful eye was kept on his lectures at the Jefferson School of Social Science, which listed its aims as education "in the spirit of democracy, peace and socialism" and taught Marxism as "the philosophy and science of the working class."[14] Hammett taught a course in mystery writing at the school and was a star guest at the second anniversary school dinner in 1946. The school had been listed as subversive by the attorney general, but the FBI report concluded that "it does not appear that the subject is engaged in deciding policy for the Communist Party."[15] Accordingly, investigation of him was suspended. The bureau's interest remained quiescent until the beginning of 1950, when a comprehensive twenty-page report listed some fifty connections between Hammett and various Communist groups or fronts.[16] Most of these references were trivial, along the lines that he had spoken at meetings, was linked with left-wing groups, and had signed an appeal for clemency on behalf of a man sentenced to a year's imprisonment for contempt of the House Un-American Activities Committee. One association, however, was to be of crucial importance, his role as president of a front organization called the Civil Rights Congress.

In spite of the twenty-page report, Hammett's political activities were muted compared with what they had been in the thirties. Because of his prestige he was a useful figurehead to serve as president of the CRC, to sign protests, to appear at meetings, and to make occasional well-publicized contributions to funds for this and that. He seems to have done little more, and it is likely that he had become doubtful of much party dogma, although he would never have made such doubts public. While in the Aleutians, Hammett had received a letter from his brother, Richard, the first communication between them for more than twenty years. When they met after the war, Richard, a conservative with a job at Standard Oil, asked him if he was a Communist. Dashiell's reply, "I'm a Marxist,"[17] is not likely to have enlightened or satisfied Richard, but for him the distinction was a real one. It was also at this time that he went to see his father and after the old man's death paid for the funeral.

In 1948 Hammett collapsed. His housekeeper, Rose Evans, called Hellman, who had not seen him for two months. They dressed him and took him to Hellman's house, where she said afterward: "That night I watched delirium tremens, although I didn't know what I was watching until the doctor told me next day at the hospital."[18] In the hospital the doctor, an old friend, told Hammett that if he went on drinking, he would be dead in a few months. Hammett promised to stop and did so, to everybody's surprise. He never drank again seriously and for a long while did not drink at all.

Not long after his recovery he was offered and accepted a Hollywood assignment to write a script for the successful play *Detective Story.* He visited his ex-wife and Jo, stayed at the house he had bought for Jose, apparently enjoyed himself. Patricia Neal was in Hollywood, and he took her out to expensive restaurants. She enjoyed the occasions, which ended with no more than a kiss, but found it hard to talk to him and thought him very old. He also met former friends, although given his taciturnity when sober, he may have had little to say. No doubt he tried to write a script for William Wyler, who had hired him, but he failed. According to one report, he returned the $10,000 advance he had been given and told Wyler that he just couldn't do it any more.[19]

What he could still do, however, was read, criticize, advise. On his return to the East from Hollywood he read the draft of Hellman's new play, *The Autumn Garden.* Her gift for dramatization of events should never be forgotten, but, according to her, his criticism was sharp and angry. She quotes him as saying: "You started as a serious writer. . . . I don't know what's happened, but tear this up and throw it away. It's worse than bad—it's half good."[20] She says that she tore up the draft accordingly (although Layman notes that an intact version labeled "first draft" still exists) and did not mention it again until she gave him the revised version seven months later. Then he told her that it was the best play anybody had written in a long time but that a speech in the last act had gone sour and should be rewritten.[21] He rewrote or revised it, and the speech has been taken as expressing much of his feeling about his own life. It is spoken by a general, "a good-looking man of fifty-three" (Hammett was a little older), who envisions a crucial moment in a man's life, the moment when "you'd suddenly wipe out your past mistakes, do the work you'd never done, think the way you'd never thought, have what you'd never had." You are either ready for that moment, the general says, or you've frittered yourself away. "I've frittered myself away."[22] The speech is in fact rather inappropriate to the general's finding himself forever tied to a woman he has never loved, and the play as a whole does not confirm Hammett's handsome words about its merits. In performance it had only moderate success, and he attributed its commercial and artistic failure to compromises made in the course of rehearsal.

The first rumblings of approaching disaster came late in 1949, when with the worsening of relations between the United States and the Soviet Union the government attitude toward the American Communist party and its fellow travelers greatly hardened. When the Civil Rights Congress used $260,000 of a large bail fund to free eleven Communists and sympathizers who were appealing their conviction for criminal conspiracy to overthrow the U.S. government by violence, the organization and its prominent supporters received much hostile press attention. In March 1950 the American Legion post in the Panama Canal Zone filed a typical protest, listing some of Hammett's Communist connections, identifying him as a fellow traveler, and requesting "that the local Armed Forces Radio Station no longer support the writings of Dashiell Hammett."[23] In July 1951, after the appeals had been denied, four of the more important Communists jumped bail, and the bail fund trustees were called to account for the background of the fund and to say anything they knew about the whereabouts of the missing men. Hammett was called as a witness, and because he refused to answer questions, was given a six-month sentence for contempt of court.

A good deal has been written, particularly by Hellman, suggesting that Hammett's stand in the matter was heroic. She has said that he went to jail because he refused to name the other contributors to the fund, and that he refused even though he had never been in the CRC offices and did not know the name of a single contributor.[24] "I can't say that," she records him as saying in answer to her question why he did not name them. He added that it had something to do with keeping his word and that "I hate this damn kind of talk, but maybe I better tell you that if it were more than jail, if it were my life, I would give it for what I think democracy is, and I don't let cops or judges tell me what I think democracy is."[25]

Perhaps he did say all this, although it sounds uncommonly like a speech from a Hellman play. In any case the truth, as revealed by the proceedings, is more humdrum.[26] It has been said that Hammett was a figurehead, but he had initialed the accounts of meetings, and it seems most unlikely that he had never been in the offices. He was not sentenced for refusal to name the contributors, something he was never directly asked to do, but because he would not answer any questions at all. He declined, always "on the ground that the answer may tend to incriminate me," to say even whether he was one of the fund's five trustees or whether the initials D. H. on documents were his or in his hand. Also pleading the Fifth Amendment, he declined to say whether he knew any of the bail-jumping Communists and whether the bail fund had a deposit box or a checkbook. It is difficult to see what the judge could have done but sentence him for contempt when confronted by this total intransigence, adhered to in spite of frequent instructions by the court to answer. High-flown language about "what democracy is" seems wholly inappropriate. The only unusual aspect of the case was the refusal of bail to Hammett, at first because CRC money was not acceptable as a bond and later at the request of the federal attorney.

He served five months in prison, first in New York's West Street detention center, where he worked in the library, later in Ashland, Kentucky. His reaction to jail Hellman found odd and often irritating: "He talked of his time there the way I remembered young men talking about their survival in a severe prep school or a tough football game,"[27] and the reaction she describes is confirmed in his letters. Going to jail, he later said, was like going home, and there seems to have been a sense in which he almost

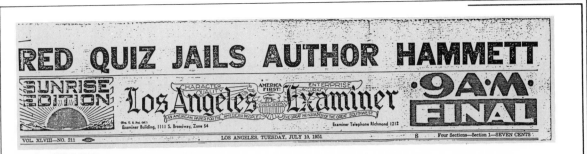

Los Angeles Examiner, *July 10, 1951*

*Hammett (center) was sentenced to prison for refusing to testify
about the CRC bail fund in U.S. District Court hearings, 1951; from
left: Joseph Orsini on unrelated narcotics charges and four CRC
trustees, W. Alphaeus Hunton, Hammett, Frederick Vanderbilt
Field, Abner Green.* (Wide World Photos)

enjoyed or at any rate accepted it, as he willingly accepted the regimentation of army life. He did the chores he was given without complaint and
joked to Hellman that he was much better at cleaning bathrooms than she
had ever been. Hardship brought out the best in him, and he felt contempt
whenever he discerned weakness. When asked why he did not like Clifford
Odets' *Awake and Sing,* he said: "Because I don't think writers who cry
about not having had a bicycle when they were kiddies are ever going to
amount to much."[28]

What he may not have realized—although it is unlikely that any prior
knowledge would have affected his attitude—is that he was a ruined man.
In the years when Senator Joseph McCarthy ruled the roost, any association with Communists, or even with the liberal causes that thousands of
people had supported in the Roosevelt era, was enough to damage the
livelihood of anybody connected with show business. A blacklist operated
in Hollywood, excluding from employment all party members and the far
more numerous fellow travelers, except those who recanted and informed.
Hammett did not recant, and he paid the penalty. His radio shows were
taken off the air; his books were not reprinted; advertisements for a revival
of a film of *The Maltese Falcon* were torn down. All of his sources of
income were removed at a stroke, and the Internal Revenue Service attached against back taxes any money that came in. Hellman had her own
troubles as the anti-Communist storm gathered and spread. After *The
Autumn Garden* she had no play produced until 1955, and then it was an
adaptation of a play by Jean Anouilh, not her original work. When she
visited Britain to work on a movie script, she was issued only a limited
passport. She had to sell Hardscrabble Farm, and although she saw
Hammett regularly, they no longer lived together. She made a list of
people who owed him money, but when she showed the list to him, he told
her not to send the letters she had drafted, because nobody would answer
them.

Almost certainly he was right. No voice was raised in protest among
his fellow writers. Some Hollywood figures were happy to avoid prosecution by branding friends and acquaintances, saying that they had been
associated with this or that protest group, had attended meetings along
with known Communists, or had given money innocently to what proved
to be Communist-front organizations. Some directors and writers went to

Hammett testifying in Senate Investigation Subcommittee headed by Joseph McCarthy, 1953 (Wide World Photos)

Europe, and others worked under pseudonyms. When Hellman wrote to Faulkner in the hope that he would sign a letter asking for Hammett's release, he did not reply. At a casual meeting with her several years later he asked after Hammett. When told that Hammett was sick he remarked only: "He drank too much."[29] Such reactions would not have surprised Hammett. Hellman was right in saying that he was a man who never expected anything from anybody. He made no complaint about his fate but settled down to live at Katonah, twenty miles north of Manhattan, in a four-room gatekeeper's cottage provided by a friend.

For the most part he was left alone, although the FBI kept an un-benevolent eye on him, and in 1953 he was called to testify again before the Senate Permanent Investigations Subcommittee headed by McCarthy. He maintained his refusal to answer any questions relating to the Communist party, invoking the Fifth Amendment as before, but sparks of the old fire were apparent when he was questioned by McCarthy and his chief counsel, Roy Cohn. When asked whether he thought American communism would be a good system for the United States, he said that the question could not be answered yes or no. The exchange continued:

THE CHAIRMAN You could not answer that "yes" or "no," whether you think communism is superior to our form of government?

HAMMETT You see, I don't understand. Theoretical communism is no form of government. You know, there is no government. And I actually don't know, and I couldn't, without—even in the end, I doubt if I could give a definite answer.

THE CHAIRMAN Would you favor the adoption of communism in this country?

HAMMETT You mean now?

THE CHAIRMAN Yes.

HAMMETT No.

THE CHAIRMAN You would not?

HAMMETT For one thing, it would seem to me impractical, if most people didn't want it.

At the end of Hammett's long session on the witness stand McCarthy asked what was meant to be a knockout question:

THE CHAIRMAN Mr. Hammett, if you were spending, as we are, over a hundred million dollars a year on an information program allegedly for the purpose of fighting communism, and if you were in charge of that program to fight communism, would you purchase the works of some 75 Communist authors and distribute their works throughout the world, placing our official stamp of approval upon those works?

Or would you rather not answer that question?

HAMMETT Well, I think—of course, I don't know—if I were fighting communism, I don't think I would do it by giving people any books at all.[30]

In due course all of Hammett's books were removed from State Department libraries.

It was in these unpromising circumstances that in 1952 Hammett made his last and most determined attempt to write another novel. The title was *Tulip*, and he completed 12,500 words of the book. After that he gave up, although he seems to have returned to the manuscript more than once and perhaps tinkered with it. The completed fragment was included in the collection *The Big Knockover*, issued in 1966. *Tulip* is interesting, although it seems unlikely that it would ever have been a successful novel. It is entirely autobiographical, going back to Hammett's life in World War I and reflecting several incidents relating both to that time and later. The narrator, called Pop, has served a short jail sentence for his political views and is a lunger. Tulip is an old army friend; Pop is working on a novel; and at one point we are offered a long review he wrote in the thirties about a book on Rosicrucianism. There is a good deal of Hemingwayesque dialogue, but it establishes little except that both Pop and Tulip are writers. The following speech by Pop is perhaps the most meaningful passage in what was written of the book. He is talking to a fourteen-year-old boy named Tony, "or perhaps through him to Tulip":

"I've been in a couple of wars—or at least in the Army while they were going on—and in federal prisons and I had t.b. for seven years and have been married as often as I chose and have had children and grandchildren and except for one fairly nice but pointless brief short story about a lunger going to Tijuana for an afternoon and evening holiday from his hospital near San Diego I've never written a word

The Big Knockover *(1966), edited by Lillian Hellman, contains*
Hammett's unfinished, last attempt at a novel, Tulip. *(UCSD)*

about any of these things. Why? All I can say is they're not for me. Maybe not yet, maybe not ever. I used to try now and then—and I suppose I tried hard, the way I tried a lot of things—but they never came out meaning very much to me."[31]

These were all fragments of Hammett's own experience, even the story about the lunger going to Tijuana, and the purpose of the book may have been to contradict Pop's contention that personal experience is of no use to a writer. The completed fiction might have been firmly based in reality, finally taking as its subject the relationship between reality and what a writer puts down on the page. A few lines which, according to Hellman, would have been at the end of the book confirm the latter idea: Pop shows the completed work to Tulip, now in the hospital, and Tulip comments: "It's all right, I guess, but you seem to have missed the point."[32] Fiction, it might be said, will always seem to miss the point for those concerned with reality, as Hammett had been during his writing life.

With *Tulip* laid aside, Hammett returned to being what he called a nice old man puttering around suburbia. He read Proust and remarked in a letter that "if he doesn't get through with Albertine pretty soon, I'm afraid he's going to lose a customer." Beyond this he did nothing: "The ugly little country cottage grew uglier with books piled on every chair and no place to sit, the desk a foot high with unanswered mail. . . . The phonograph was unplayed, the typewriter untouched, the beloved, foolish gadgets unopened in their packages."[33] At one of Hellman's weekly visits he said that he had been falling down, couldn't live alone any longer, and would go into a veterans' hospital. She persuaded him not to go to the veterans' hospital, and he lived for part of the time in a house she had bought on Martha's Vineyard, although he retained the Katonah cottage.

In 1955 he had a heart attack and was granted a total disability pension. Early in 1957 the FBI, still on the alert, noted that he had contributed one dollar to the American Committee for the Protection of the Foreign Born and had signed a resolution condemning armed aggression against Guatemala. In May of that year he was interviewed. "Subject stated he has been very sick for several years, was still of the same opinion as when he appeared before the Senate Committee, and stated he did not care to discuss his own activities."[34] (He was still teaching a mystery-writing course at the Jefferson School.) He further said that he was unemployed, had no

Hammett after 1955 (New York *Daily News*)

income, received no royalties, and lived rent-free. He explained to the interviewer that he had started a book some years ago but had done nothing for the past couple of years. He knew of no money owed to him and had no reason to anticipate any change in his financial position. He was therefore unable to pay any of the $140,795 he owed to the Internal Revenue Service.

In the same year a journalist came to the cottage. He found Hammett still in pajamas at noon, "a lean 6 foot man with bushy hair, startlingly white in contrast to his black scars of eyebrows and moustache." He noted the three typewriters, "mute as tombstones." Why three? "I keep them chiefly to remind myself that I was once a writer." This ironic tone was maintained throughout the interview. Hammett said that he was content to do no more than cook for himself and bring in wood for the log fire. "I am concentrating on my health," he said. "I am learning to be a hypochondriac." He said he had stopped writing because he found he was repeating himself. "It is the beginning of the end when you discover you have style," he said rather enigmatically, adding that what had really ruined him was writing the last third of *The Glass Key* in a single thirty-hour sitting. And why hadn't he written in jail? "I was never bored enough."[35]

It is to be hoped that Hammett enjoyed this interview, for there can have been little in these last years that gave him pleasure. After he left prison he did not buy a suit or tie until Hellman's first wholly original play in nine years, *Toys in the Attic*, opened in New York. For that he bought new dinner clothes. But his last two or three years were lived through painfully. He died on 10 January 1961, at the age of sixty-six. The cause of death was a cancerous tumor in the right lung. He also had emphysema and a diseased heart, liver, kidneys, spleen, and prostate.

The memorial service was attended by three hundred people, including Dorothy Parker, Patricia Neal, and Lionel Trilling. A eulogy was delivered by Hellman: "He believed in the salvation of intelligence. . . . He didn't always think very well of the society we live in, and yet when it punished him he made no complaint against it, and had no anger about the punishment."[36] Those are true words. He was buried, as he had wished, at Arlington National Cemetery.

NOTES

CHAPTER ONE

1. John Ward Ostrom, ed., *Letters of Edgar Allan Poe*, vol. 2 (Cambridge: Harvard University Press, 1966), p. 328.

2. Raymond Chandler, "The Simple Art of Murder," *Atlantic Monthly*, December 1944, pp. 53–59.

CHAPTER TWO

1. Dashiell Hammett, untitled letter, *The Black Mask*, November 1924, p. 128.

2. Richard Layman, *Shadow Man: The Life of Dashiell Hammett* (New York & London: Harcourt Brace Jovanovich, 1981), p. 4.

3. Ibid., pp. 7–8.

4. Richard Hammett to Walter Godschalk, 1 April 1974.

5. Interview in *New York Evening Journal*. Unlocated 1934 clipping.

6. Dashiell Hammett, "From the Memoirs of a Private Detective," *The Smart Set*, March 1923, pp. 88–90.

7. Phil Haultain, "Dashiell Hammett's San Francisco: Phil Haultain Looks

Back," *City of San Francisco*, 4 November 1975, p. 34.

8. Ibid., p. 38.
9. Ibid.
10. Ibid.
11. Diane Johnson, *Dashiell Hammett: A Life* (New York: Random House, 1983), p. 308.
12. Ibid., p. 36.

CHAPTER THREE

1. Dashiell Hammett, "The Need for Tempo in the Contemporary Novel," typescript, Bancroft Library, University of California, Berkeley.
2. Dashiell Hammett, "The Great Lovers," *The Smart Set*, November 1922, p. 4.
3. Dashiell Hammett, *Dead Yellow Women*, ed. Ellery Queen (New York: Spivak, 1946), pp. 94–95.
4. Dashiell Hammett, *The Big Knockover*, ed. Lillian Hellman (New York: Random House, 1966), pp. 28–29.
5. Ibid., p. 29.
6. Ibid., p. 31.
7. Hammett, *Dead Yellow Women*, p. 81.
8. Dashiell Hammett, *The Continental Op*, ed. Steven Marcus (New York: Random House, 1974), p. 160.
9. Ibid., p. 92.
10. Hammett, *The Big Knockover*, pp. 172, 210, 228.
11. Ibid., p. 191.
12. Dashiell Hammett, letter in *The Black Mask*, June 1924.
13. Ibid.
14. David Fechheimer, "Mrs. Hammett Is Alive and Well in L.A.," *City of San Francisco*, 4 November 1975, p. 38.
15. Steven Marcus, "Introduction," in Dashiell Hammett, *The Continental Op*, p. xx.
16. Hammett, *The Continental Op*, p. 197.
17. Hammett, *The Big Knockover*, p. 235.
18. Ibid., p. 221.
19. Ibid., pp. 217–218.
20. Ibid., pp. vii–viii.
21. Larry Levinger, "My Father Liked Precision: The Samuels Story," *City of San Francisco*, 4 November 1975, p. 24.
22. Ibid.
23. William F. Nolan, *Hammett: A Life at the Edge* (New York: Congdon & Weed, 1983), p. 63.

24. Levinger, *City of San Francisco*, p. 24.
25. Johnson, *Dashiell Hammett*, p. 65.
26. Layman, *Shadow Man*, p. 76.
27. Nolan, *A Life at the Edge*, pp. 61–62.
28. Joseph T. Shaw, "Introduction," in Dashiell Hammett, *The Hard-Boiled Omnibus*, ed. Joseph T. Shaw (New York: Simon & Schuster, 1946), p. vi.
29. Fechheimer, *City of San Francisco*, p. 38.
30. Hammett, "The Big Knockover," *The Big Knockover*, pp. 289–290.
31. Hammett, "$106,000 Blood Money," *The Big Knockover*, p. 321.
32. Hammett, "The Big Knockover," *The Big Knockover*, p. 307.
33. Hammett, "$106,000 Blood Money," *The Big Knockover*, p. 337.

CHAPTER FOUR
1. Layman, *Shadow Man*, p. 89.
2. Dashiell Hammett, *Red Harvest* (New York & London: Knopf, 1929), p. 11.
3. Ibid., pp. 15–16.
4. Ibid., p. 13.
5. Ibid., p. 39.
6. Ibid., pp. 193, 197.
7. Leslie Fiedler, *Love and Death in the American Novel* (New York: Criterion Books, 1960), p. 476.
8. Hammett, *Red Harvest*, p. 80.
9. Ibid., pp. 255–256.
10. Chandler, "The Simple Art of Murder," pp. 53–59.
11. Hammett, *Red Harvest*, 86–93.
12. Ibid., p. 70.
13. Johnson, *Dashiell Hammett*, p. 69.
14. Ibid., p. 70.
15. Layman, *Shadow Man*, p. 80.
16. Ibid., pp. 70–71.
17. Johnson, *Dashiell Hammett*, p. 72.
18. Layman, *Shadow Man*, p. 97.
19. Cyril Connolly, *The Condemned Playground: Essays 1927–1944* (London: Routledge, 1945), p. 102.
20. André Gide, *The Journals of André Gide*, vol. 4, trans. Justin O'Brien (New York: Knopf, 1951), p. 191.
21. Edmund Wilson, *Classics and Commercials* (New York: Farrar, Straus, 1950), pp. 235–236.
22. A. Alvarez, *Beyond All This Fiddle, Essays 1955–1967* (New York: Random House, 1969), p. 212.

23. Dashiell Hammett, *The Dain Curse* (New York & London: Knopf, 1929), p. 20.
24. Ibid.
25. John Bartlow Martin, "Peekaboo Pennington, Private Eye," *Harper's*, May 1946, pp. 450–461; see Nolan, *A Life at the Edge*, p. 80.
26. *Black Mask*, November 1928, p. 67.
27. Hammett, *The Dain Curse*, p. 254.
28. Ibid., p. 22.
29. Ibid., p. 207.
30. Ibid., p. 74. Original text in *Black Mask*, November 1928, pp. 41–67.
31. Layman, *Shadow Man*, pp. 86–87.
32. Nolan, *A Life at the Edge*, p. 97.
33. Layman, *Shadow Man*, p. 106.

CHAPTER FIVE

1. Dashiell Hammett, "Introduction," *The Maltese Falcon* (New York: Modern Library, 1934), pp. vii–viii.
2. Dust-jacket blurb on first edition of Hammett, *The Glass Key* (New York: Knopf, 1931); Franklin P. Adams, *The Diary of Our Own Samuel Pepys*, vol. 2 (New York: Simon & Schuster, 1935), p. 961; see Layman, *Shadow Man*, pp. 112–113.
3. "Crime Wave," *New York Evening Post*, 7 June 1930, S4; see Layman, *Shadow Man*, pp. 122–123.
4. Ibid., 3 July 1930, S5; see Layman, *Shadow Man*, p. 123.
5. Ibid., 19 July 1930, S5.
6. Dashiell Hammett, *The Maltese Falcon* (New York & London: Knopf, 1930), p. 3.
7. Ibid., p. 264.
8. Ibid., pp. 213–214.
9. Ibid., p. 40.
10. Ibid., p. 127.
11. Ibid., p. 114.
12. Ibid., p. 70.
13. Ibid., pp. 111–112.
14. Ibid., p. 263.
15. Johnson, *Dashiell Hammett*, p. 77.
16. Ibid., p. 78.
17. Hammett, *The Maltese Falcon*, p. 83.
18. Ibid., p. 115.
19. Ibid., p. 145.
20. Ibid., p. 133.

21. Hammett, *Dead Yellow Women*, p. 197.
22. Hammett, *The Maltese Falcon*, p. 256.
23. Nolan, *A Life at the Edge*, p. 200.
24. Hammett, *The Maltese Falcon*, p. 138.
25. Ibid., p. 147.
26. Ibid., pp. 21–30.
27. Ross Macdonald, "Homage to Dashiell Hammett," in *Self-Portrait* (Santa Barbara, Calif.: Capra Press, 1981), pp. 111–112.
28. Robert I. Edenbaum, "The Poetics of the Private-Eye: The Novels of Dashiell Hammett," in *Tough Guy Writers of the Thirties*, ed. David Madden (Carbondale: Southern Illinois University Press, 1968), p. 83.
29. Layman, *Shadow Man*, p. 112.
30. John Cawelti, *Adventure, Mystery, and Romance* (Chicago: University of Chicago Press, 1976), p. 167.
31. William Ruehlmann, *Saint With a Gun: The Unlawful American Private Eye* (New York: New York University Press, 1974), p. 74.
32. George J. Thompson, "The Problem of Moral Vision in Dashiell Hammett's Detective Novels," *Armchair Detective*, May 1974, p. 183.
33. Lillian Hellman, *Pentimento* (Boston & Toronto: Little, Brown, 1973), p. 278.

CHAPTER SIX
1. Layman, *Shadow Man*, p. 126.
2. Ibid., p. 130.
3. Lillian Hellman, *An Unfinished Woman* (Boston & Toronto: Little, Brown, 1969), pp. 258–259.
4. Ibid., p. 259.
5. Ibid.
6. Hellman, *Pentimento*, p. 14.
7. Ibid., p. 97.
8. Ibid., p. 160.
9. Johnson, *Dashiell Hammett*, pp. 100–101.
10. Dashiell Hammett, "On the Way," *Harper's Bazaar*, March 1932, pp. 44–45.

CHAPTER SEVEN
1. Elizabeth Sanderson, "Ex-Detective Hammett," *Bookman*, January–February 1932, pp. 517–518.
2. Dorothy Parker, "Oh Look—Two Good Books," *New Yorker*, 25 April 1931, p. 91.
3. Nolan, *A Life at the Edge*, p. 98.
4. Dashiell Hammett, *The Glass Key* (New York & London: Knopf, 1931), p. 10.

5. Ibid., p. 30.

6. Ibid., p. 90.

7. Ibid., p. 84.

8. Ibid., pp. 195, 200.

9. Ibid., p. 114.

10. Ibid., p. 119.

11. Ibid., p. 243.

12. James Cooper, "Lean Years for This Thin Man," *Washington Daily News*, 11 March 1957.

13. Hammett, *The Glass Key*, pp. 167–168.

14. Ibid., p. 212.

15. Ibid., p. 280.

16. Ibid., p. 234.

17. Ibid., p. 278.

18. The text does not seem to me to justify the view that Beaumont had sexual connection with Eloise Mathews (*The Glass Key*, pp. 171–173).

19. Nolan, *A Life at the Edge*, p. 101.

CHAPTER EIGHT

1. Joseph Blotner, *Faulkner, a Biography* (New York: Random House, 1974), pp. 740–743.

2. Interview, *New York Evening Journal*. Unlocated 1934 clipping.

3. Hammett, "Thin Man" supplement, *City of San Francisco*, p. 1. This is the only complete printing.

4. Layman, *Shadow Man*, p. 131.

5. Hammett, "Thin Man" supplement, *City of San Francisco*, p. 12.

6. Ibid.

7. Dashiell Hammett to Lillian Hellman, 30 April 1931; Johnson, *Dashiell Hammett*, pp. 101–102.

8. Dashiell Hammett, "A Man Called Spade," *American Magazine*, July 1932, pp. 32–36, 92, 94–100.

9. Dashiell Hammett, "They Can Only Hang You Once," *Collier's*, November 1932, pp. 22–24.

10. Dashiell Hammett, "Night Shade," *Mystery League Magazine*, 1 October 1933; "Albert Pastor at Home," *Esquire*, Autumn 1933, p. 34.

11. Hellman, *An Unfinished Woman*, p. 270.

12. Ibid.

13. Dashiell Hammett, *The Thin Man* (New York: Knopf, 1934), p. 37.

14. Hellman, *An Unfinished Woman*, p. 270.

15. Hammett, *The Thin Man*, p. 136.

16. Ibid.
17. Ibid., p. 142.
18. Ibid., p. 153.
19. Ibid., p. 112.
20. Ibid., p. 259.
21. Carl Van Vechten, *Parties* (New York: Knopf, 1930), p. 37.
22. Ibid., p. 30.
23. Hammett, *The Thin Man*, p. 86.
24. Edenbaum, "The Poetics of the Private-Eye," p. 102.
25. Hammett, *The Thin Man*, p. 164.
26. Ibid., p. 117.
27. Ibid., p. 192.
28. Advertisement, *New York Times*, 30 January 1934; see Layman, *Shadow Man*, p. 145.

CHAPTER NINE

1. "Author of Thrillers Is Sorry He Killed His Book Character," *San Francisco Call Bulletin*, 3 November 1934; see Nolan, *A Life at the Edge*, p. 146.
2. "Author of Thrillers," p. 140.
3. Hammett's FBI file.
4. Layman, *Shadow Man*, p. 159.
5. Nolan, *A Life at the Edge*, p. 147.
6. Jay Martin, *Nathanael West: The Art of His Life* (New York: Farrar, Straus & Giroux, 1970), p. 268.
7. John Carr, "An Interview with James M. Cain," *Armchair Detective*, 1983, p. 12.
8. Johnson, *Dashiell Hammett*, pp. 122–123.
9. Raymond Chandler to Alex Barris, 16 April 1949, *Selected Letters of Raymond Chandler*, ed. Frank MacShane (New York: Columbia University Press, 1981), p. 165.
10. Dashiell Hammett, "His Brother's Keeper," *Collier's*, February 1934, pp. 10–11.
11. Hellman, *Pentimento*, pp. 172–173.
12. Hellman, *An Unfinished Woman*, p. 272.
13. James Thurber, "The Wings of Henry James," in *Lanterns & Lances* (Alexandria, Va: Time-Life, 1962), p. 77.
14. "The Films Now Know Miss Hellman," *New York Herald Tribune*, 7 July 1935, V3.
15. Hellman, *Pentimento*, p. 161.
16. Henry Dan Piper, "Dashiel [*sic*] Hammett Flees Night Club Round Succumb-

ing to Rustication in New Jersey," *Daily Princetonian,* 11 November 1936, pp. 1, 4; see Layman, *Shadow Man,* pp. 164–165.

CHAPTER TEN

1. Nunnally Johnson to Julian Symons, 16 January 1961. Quoted in *Letters of Nunnally Johnson,* ed. Dorris Johnson and Ellen Leventhal (New York: Knopf, 1981), pp. 187–188.
2. Dashiell Hammett to Lillian Hellman, 26 December 1937; see Johnson, *Dashiell Hammett,* p. 145.
3. Van Vechten, *Parties,* p. 285.
4. Hellman, *An Unfinished Woman,* p. 69.
5. Ibid., p. 70.
6. Ibid., pp. 71–72.
7. Layman, *Shadow Man,* p. 173.
8. Hellman, *An Unfinished Woman,* p. 74.
9. Johnson, *Dashiell Hammett,* p. 142.
10. Hellman, *Pentimento,* p. 172.
11. Ibid.
12. Bernard F. Dick, *Hellman in Hollywood* (Hackensack, N.J.: Fairleigh Dickinson University Press, 1982), pp. 88–92.
13. Hammett's FBI file.
14. Ibid.
15. Ibid.
16. Ibid.
17. Ibid.

CHAPTER ELEVEN

1. Layman, *Shadow Man,* p. 189.
2. Hellman, *An Unfinished Woman,* p. 257.
3. Dashiell Hammett to Lillian Hellman, 25 October 1943; see Johnson, *Dashiell Hammett,* p. 180.
4. Nolan, *A Life at the Edge,* pp. 188–189.
5. Johnson, *Dashiell Hammett,* p. 195.
6. Ibid., p. 194.
7. Layman, *Shadow Man,* 192.
8. Nolan, *A Life at the Edge,* p. 189.
9. Ibid., p. 190.
10. Hammett's FBI file.
11. Johnson, *Dashiell Hammett,* p. 218.
12. Ibid., p. 221.

13. Hammett's FBI file.
14. Layman, *Shadow Man,* p. 206.
15. Hammett's FBI file.
16. These are listed in detail in Layman, *Shadow Man,* pp. 206–210.
17. Layman, *Shadow Man,* p. 215.
18. Hellman, *An Unfinished Woman,* p. 261.
19. Nolan, *A Life at the Edge,* p. 212.
20. Hellman, *An Unfinished Woman,* pp. 267–268.
21. Ibid., p. 268.
22. Lillian Hellman, *The Autumn Garden* (Boston: Little, Brown, 1951), pp. 133–134.
23. Hammett's FBI file.
24. Hellman, *An Unfinished Woman,* p. 261.
25. Ibid., p. 262.
26. The proceedings are printed in full in Layman, *Shadow Man,* pp. 248–262.
27. Lillian Hellman, *Scoundrel Time* (Boston & Toronto: Little, Brown, 1976), p. 49.
28. Ibid., p. 65.
29. Blotner, *Faulkner, a Biography,* p. 1666.
30. For a detailed account, see Layman, *Shadow Man,* pp. 225–232.
31. Hammett, *The Big Knockover,* pp. 261–262.
32. Ibid., p. 274.
33. Hellman, *An Unfinished Woman,* p. 277.
34. Hammett's FBI file.
35. Cooper, "Lean Years for This Thin Man."
36. Nolan, *A Life at the Edge,* p. 237.

BIBLIOGRAPHY

COMPILED BY JUDITH BAUGHMAN

Primary

BOOKS

Red Harvest. New York & London: Knopf, 1929.

The Dain Curse. New York & London: Knopf, 1929; London & New York: Knopf, 1930.

The Maltese Falcon. New York & London: Knopf, 1930; London & New York: Knopf, 1930.

The Glass Key. London & New York: Knopf, 1931; New York & London: Knopf, 1931.

Creeps by Night. Edited by Dashiell Hammett. New York: Day, 1931. Republished as *Modern Tales of Horror* (London: Gollancz, 1932).

The Thin Man. New York: Knopf, 1934; London: Barker, 1935.

Secret Agent X–9, Book 1. Philadelphia: McKay, 1934. Comic strip.

Secret Agent X–9, Book 2. Philadelphia: McKay, 1934. Comic strip.

$106,000 Blood Money. New York: Spivak, 1943. Includes "The Big Knockover" and "$106,000 Blood Money."

The Battle of the Aleutians, by Dashiell Hammett and Robert Colodny. Adak, Alaska: Intelligence Section, Field Force Headquarters, Adak, 1944.

The Adventures of Sam Spade and Other Stories. New York: Spivak, 1944. Includes "Too Many Have Lived," "They Can Only Hang You Once," "A Man Called Spade," "The Assistant Murderer," "Nightshade," "The Judge Laughed Last," and "His Brother's Keeper." Republished as *They Can Only Hang You Once* (New York: Spivak/Mercury Mystery, 1949).

The Continental Op. New York: Spivak, 1945. Includes "Fly Paper," "Death on Pine Street," "Zigzags of Treachery," and "The Farewell Murder."

The Return of the Continental Op. New York: Spivak, 1945. Includes "The Whosis Kid," "The Gutting of Couffignal," "Death and Company," "One Hour," and "The Tenth Clue."

Hammett Homicides. New York: Spivak, 1946. Includes "The House in Turk Street," "The Girl with the Silver Eyes," "Night Shots," "The Main Death," "Two Sharp Knives," and "Ruffian's Wife."

Dead Yellow Women. New York: Spivak, 1947. Includes "Dead Yellow Women," "The Golden Horseshoe," "House Dick," "Who Killed Bob Teal?" "The Green Elephant," and "The Hairy One."

Nightmare Town. Edited by Ellery Queen. New York: Spivak/Mercury Mystery, 1948. Includes "Nightmare Town," "The Scorched Face," "Albert Pastor at Home," and "Corkscrew."

The Creeping Siamese. Edited by Ellery Queen. New York: Spivak, 1950. Includes "The Creeping Siamese," "The Man Who Killed Dan Odams," "The Nails in Mr. Cayterer," "The Joke on Eloise Morey," "Tom, Dick or Harry," and "This King Business."

The Woman in the Dark. Edited by Ellery Queen. New York: Spivak, 1951. Includes "Arson Plus," "Slippery Fingers," "The Black Hat That Wasn't There," "Woman in the Dark," "Afraid of a Gun," "Holiday," and "The Man Who Stood in the Way."

A Man Named Thin and Other Stories. Edited by Ellery Queen. New York: Ferman, 1962. Includes "A Man Named Thin," "Wages of Crime," "The Gatewood Caper," "The Barber and His Wife," "Itchy the Debonair," "The Second-Story Angel," "In the Morgue," and "When Luck's Running Good."

The Big Knockover. Edited by Lillian Hellman. New York: Random House, 1966; London: Cassell, 1966. Includes "The Gutting of Couffignal," "Fly Paper," "The Scorched Face," "This King Business," "The Gatewood Caper," "Dead

Yellow Women," "Corkscrew," "Tulip," "The Big Knockover," and "$106,000 Blood Money."

The Continental Op. Edited by Steven Marcus. New York: Random House, 1974. Includes "The Tenth Clew," "The Golden Horseshoe," "The House in Turk Street," "The Girl with the Silver Eyes," "The Whosis Kid," "The Main Death," and "The Farewell Murder."

COLLECTIONS

Dashiell Hammett Omnibus. New York: Knopf, 1935. *Red Harvest, The Dain Curse,* and *The Maltese Falcon.*

The Dashiell Hammett Omnibus. London, Toronto, Melbourne, Sydney, Wellington: Cassell, 1950. *Red Harvest,* "Dead Yellow Women," *The Dain Curse,* "The Golden Horseshoe," *The Maltese Falcon,* "House Dick," *The Glass Key,* "Who Killed Bob Teal?" and *The Thin Man.*

The Novels of Dashiell Hammett. New York: Knopf, 1965. *Red Harvest, The Dain Curse, The Maltese Falcon, The Glass Key,* and *The Thin Man.*

Secondary

BIBLIOGRAPHY

Layman, Richard. *Dashiell Hammett: A Descriptive Bibliography.* Pittsburgh: University of Pittsburgh Press, 1979.

Nolan, William F. "The Hammett Checklist Revisited." *Armchair Detective,* August 1973, pp. 249–254.

———. "Revisiting the Revisited Hammett Checklist." *Armchair Detective,* October 1976, pp. 292–295, 324–329.

Biographical and Critical Works

Adams, Donald K. "The First Thin Man." In *The Mystery and Detection Annual.* Vol. 1, pp. 160–177. Beverly Hills, Calif.: Adams, 1972.

"Author of Thrillers Is Sorry He Killed His Book Character," *San Francisco Call Bulletin,* 3 November 1934.

Bazelon, David T. "Dashiell Hammett's Private Eye." In *The Scene before You: A New Approach to American Culture,* edited by Chandler Brossard, pp. 180–190. New York: Rinehart, 1955.

Blair, Walter. "Dashiell Hammett, Themes and Techniques." In *Essays on American Literature in Honor of Jay B. Hubbell,* edited by C. Gohdes, pp. 295–306. Durham, N.C.: Duke University Press, 1967.

Chandler, Raymond. "The Simple Art of Murder." *Atlantic Monthly*, December 1944, pp. 53–59.

City of San Francisco, 4 November 1975. Hammett issue.

Cooper, James. "Lean Years for This Thin Man," *Washington Daily News*, 11 March 1957.

Dick, Bernard F. *Hellman in Hollywood*. Hackensack, N.J.: Fairleigh Dickinson University Press, 1982.

Edenbaum, Robert I. "The Poetics of the Private-Eye: The Novels of Dashiell Hammett." In *Tough Guy Writers of the Thirties*, edited by David Madden, pp. 80–103. Carbondale: Southern Illinois University Press, 1968.

Grella, George. "The Wings of the Falcon and the Maltese Dove." In *A Question of Quality*, edited by L. Filler, pp. 108–114. Bowling Green, Ohio: Bowling Green University Popular Press, 1976.

Hellman, Lillian. *Pentimento*. Boston & Toronto: Little, Brown, 1973.

———. *Scoundrel Time*. Boston & Toronto: Little, Brown, 1976.

———. *Three*. Boston & Toronto: Little, Brown, 1979. Includes *Pentimento, An Unfinished Woman*, and *Scoundrel Time*.

———. *An Unfinished Woman*. Boston & Toronto: Little, Brown, 1969.

Johnson, Diane. *Dashiell Hammett: A Life*. New York: Random House, 1983.

Layman, Richard. *Shadow Man: The Life of Dashiell Hammett*. New York & London: Harcourt Brace Jovanovich/Bruccoli Clark, 1981.

Macdonald, Ross. "Homage to Dashiell Hammett." In *Self-Portrait: Ceaselessly into the Past*. Santa Barbara, Calif.: Capra, 1981.

Malin, Irving. "Focus on 'The Maltese Falcon': The Metaphysical Falcon." In *Tough Guy Writers of the Thirties*, edited by David Madden, pp. 104–109. Carbondale: Southern Illinois University Press, 1968.

Nolan, William F. *Dashiell Hammett: A Casebook*. Santa Barbara, Calif.: McNally & Loftin, 1969.

———. *Hammett: A Life at the Edge*. New York: Congdon & Weed, 1983.

Piper, Henry Dan. "Dashiel [*sic*] Hammett Flees Night Club Round Succumbing to Rustication in New Jersey." *Daily Princetonian*, 11 November 1936, pp. 1, 4.

Ruehlmann, William. *Saint with a Gun: The Unlawful American Private Eye*. New York: New York University Press, 1974.

Sanderson, Elizabeth. "Ex-Detective Hammett." *Bookman*, January–February 1932, pp. 517–518.

Shaw, Joseph T., ed. *The Hard-Boiled Omnibus*. New York: Simon & Schuster, 1946.

Symons, Julian. "Dashiell Hammett: The Onlie Begetter." In *Crime Writers*, edited by H. R. F. Keating, pp. 80–93. London: BBC, 1978.

Thompson, George J. "The Problem of Moral Vision in Dashiell Hammett's Detective Novels." *Armchair Detective*, May, August, November 1973; May, August, November 1974; February 1975.

Van Vechten, Carl. *Parties*. New York: Knopf, 1930.

Wolfe, Peter. *Beams Falling: The Art of Dashiell Hammett*. Bowling Green, Ohio: Bowling Green University Popular Press, 1980.

INDEX